White Elephant Stampede

Case Studies in Policy and Project Management Failures

Edited by David Gration, Bruce Kingston and Scott Prasser

Connor Court Publishing

Published in 2022 by Connor Court Publishing Pty Ltd

Connor Court Publishing Pty Ltd
PO Box 7257
Redland Bay QLD 4165
sales@connorcourt.com
www.connorcourtpublishing.com.au
Phone 0497-900-685

Printed in Australia

ISBN: 9781922815187

Front Cover Image and Cover Design by Renee Gorman.

Printed in Australia

white elephant;

(noun) a possession that is useless or troublesome, especially one that is expensive to maintain or difficult to dispose of.

(Lexico.com)

CONTENTS

CONTRIBUTORS

Gary Banks AO (PhD) is a Professorial Fellow at the Melbourne Institute and Senior Fellow at the CIS. His contributions to public policy have been recognised through the Economic Society's Distinguished Public Policy Fellows Award and the Order of Australia. Gary spent nearly 15 years heading Australia's Productivity Commission, following which he was appointed Dean of ANZSOG. (*Foreword*)

Simon Dawkins (PhD) is the Executive Director of the Oil Mallee Association of Australia and Chair of TEDx Perth and Tura New Music. Simon held the position of Adjunct Associate Professor at the Curtin University Sustainability Policy Institute. Simon was a member of the UWA Senate for 11 years until 2021. (*Case Study 3*)

Brian Dollery (PhD) is Emeritus Professor of Economics at the University of New England. He has published extensively on Australian local government and worked with numerous local councils across Australia and New Zealand. His most recent co-authored book is Local Public, Fiscal and Financial Governance (Palgrave McMillan, New York, 2020). (*Case Study 4*)

Henrico Dolfing helps C-level executives in the financial service industry with interim management and recovering troubled technology projects. He has done project reviews, recoveries and advisory for over a decade, and has worked in the trenches of software development for more than 15 years. (*Case Study 6*)

David Gration (PhD) is an events researcher and mentor with over 30 years of industry experience managing services and projects in arts, events and tourism. After completing an MBA (QUT), David achieved his PhD (UQ) focusing on Festival/Event Marketing and Tourism. David is a life member of Performing Arts Connections Australia. (*Book Co-editor & Case Study 10*)

Paul Hooper (PhD) has a career spanning five decades in government, the International Civil Aviation Organization, consulting and universities. He is highly respected as an aviation economist and has published extensively. He specialises in aviation and provides advice to clients on matters such as private financing of infrastructure, business cases, and strategic planning. (*Case Study 8*)

Binoy Kampmark (PhD) is a Senior Lecturer in the School of Global, Urban and Social Studies, RMIT University. He is a contributing editor to Counter Punch, a columnist for The Mandarin, and a former Commonwealth Scholar, Selwyn College, University of Cambridge. (*Case Study 9*)

Aynsley Kellow (PhD) is Professor Emeritus of Government, University of Tasmania. Recent research is focused on international climate change negotiations, the OECD, global governance on these and similar areas. Aynsley is particularly interested in the processes by which more effective multilateral environmental agreements can be developed. (*Policy & Projects Overview*)

Bruce Kingston has some 40 years' experience in management, marketing, community engagement and public affairs roles in corporate, consulting and government roles working in various States and Territories. He has also been a University lecturer, a speechwriter, and political campaign consultant. (*Book Co-editor & Case Study 1*)

Justin Macdonnell has worked in arts management for over 50 years of holding senior executive positions in Australia, New Zealand and the USA. Justin has produced scores of reports for government and the private sector. Author of 'Arts, Minister', Justin is Executive Director of Anzarts Institute, a consultancy and think tank in the cultural industries. (*Case Study 5*)

Scott Prasser PhD has worked in federal and state governments in senior research and policy roles as well as working in academia. He has written extensively on Australian government and politics and the 2nd edition of his *Royal Commissions and Public Inquiries in Australia* was published in 2021. (*Book Co-editor & Lessons from the Stampede*)

Nadeem Samnakay (PhD), is an environment and sustainability policy researcher and practitioner. He has researched Australia's national environmental reform policies from the lens of policy processes and understanding success factors. For the past 30 years he has worked in numerous areas of environment and resource management nationally and internationally. (*Case Study 2*)

Steven Schwartz AM (PhD) is the former Vice Chancellor (President) of 3 universities in Australia and the UK. He was Chair of the Board of the Fulbright Commission and the Australian Curriculum, Assessment and Reporting Authority. He is the author of 14 books and hundreds of articles. (*Case Studies 8 & Dessert*)

FOREWORD

White Elephant Stampede -

Case Studies in Policy and Project Management Failures

Professor Gary Banks AO

The elephant could be said to have earned a special place in the lexicon of public policy.

There is for example the well-known *'elephant in the room'*, invariably called upon when policy discussions get sidetracked or lose their way (as is frequently the case). And there is the tale of the blind men who, on touching different parts of an elephant, come to different conclusions about what sort of beast they are dealing with. Policy initiatives similarly can be viewed quite differently depending on the standpoint of the decision-maker or 'stakeholder'.

Then of course there is the *white elephant,* the subject of this informative and entertaining volume.

As readers will find, 'white elephants' come in different forms, but they share a number of features in common. Not least among these is the gulf between ambition and outcome, and the sheer waste of money involved. We find repeatedly that need or demand is greatly over-estimated; costs greatly under-estimated. Yet, true to the ancient origins of the saying from the Kingdom of Siam, a white elephant once created is not easily relinquished. Its costs can endure.

Public capital investments provide some of the best-known examples: underutilized railways, mothballed desalination plants, vacant technology parks and expensive misfires in defense procurement being among my personal favourites. But there are other examples too, particularly within the regulatory realm and in the fertile territory of international 'events'. Indeed, if interpreted liberally to include any initiative for which costs greatly exceed benefits, white elephants appear everywhere!

While this phenomenon is most common in the public sector, it is not unknown in the private sector. However, the forces of profit-seeking and market competition clearly provide a much less hospitable environment there compared to the forces of *political* competition that pervade the public sector.

Does this matter? Should we be much concerned about the white elephant phenomenon? The short answer is 'yes we should - more than ever'.

Once it was possible in policy circles to get a laugh by repeating the aphorism attributed to Everett Dirksen last century that 'a billion dollars here and a billion dollars there and pretty soon you're talking real money!' But billion dollar outlays have become so commonplace that the joke seems to have lost its resonance. Australia's white elephants have been growing greatly in size, particularly since the Global Financial Crisis and the COVID pandemic.

The advent of perceived 'easy money' and the politics of catastrophe, have seen a greater willingness by governments to spend up big and regulate harder, but with less inclination than before to do the hard yards involved in sound 'evidence-based' policy making. The result has been burgeoning public expenditure, deficits and debt, with little to show for it.

Yet the need for well-targeted public spending to address deficiencies in areas such as health services and aged care remains great, highlighted by the failures observed during the current pandemic. And devoting a larger share of GDP to defense will make little difference if the money continues to be spent as poorly as it has been. (The lamentable submarine saga is addressed in this volume).

In short, white elephants do not just waste resources, they crowd out policies that would yield real benefits to society. The $64 billion question is how to stop them propagating. There are no signs of this happening at present – quite the contrary. What does seem clear is that the more information that is made publicly available about their costs and deficiencies, the less likely it is that white elephants will flourish. This volume makes a very useful contribution to that important endeavour.

POLICY AND PROJECTS OVERVIEW

Spilt Milk, Cherry Trees and White Elephants:

Rationality and Veracity in the Policy Process.

Aynsley Kellow

> 'I can't tell a lie, Pa; you know I can't tell a lie. I did cut it with my hatchet.' 'Run to my arms you dearest boy,' cried his father in transports, 'run to my arms; glad am I, George, that you killed my tree; for you have paid me for it a thousand fold.' (Weems, 1962, p. 12)

Policy studies prides itself on its interdisciplinarity. It seeks to reinject politics into economics by reminding economic policy analysts of the need to consider political factors if they are to offer useful policy advice; it similarly seeks to reinject economics and sociology into political science by reminding the political scientist of some of the motivations underlying political behaviour.

Those working in policy studies are therefore used to finding common ground with colleagues in other disciplines, at borrowing insights overlooked by others in our disciplines. Political scientists have eagerly adopted the insights of economic theorists such as Mancur Olson (1965) and Anthony Downs (1957) and have found the arguments in favour of the 'political rationality' of incrementalism advanced by Charles Lindblom (1959) to be stimulating rather than problematic.

What, then, are we to make of the following two passages from some of the foundational literature in the field? First,

Thomas R. Dye (1981, p.35): 'Large investments in existing programs and policies ("sunk costs") prevent policy-makers from reconsidering alternatives foreclosed by previous decisions'. This is advanced by Dye as one reason why policy makers might depart from rational modes of policy-making; the picture is of sunk costs counting for a lot in policy-making (at least from a political science perspective).

Contrast Dye's view, however, with that of E. S. Quade writing from a viewpoint which Richard Simeon (Simeon, 1976) characterised as 'policy analysis' rather than 'policy theory':

> Past costs are sunk costs, and the analyst must be careful not to include any sunk costs into his cost estimates. Sunk costs do not represent alternatives that we can do anything about, and hence they are no longer real costs. The costs that are important are future costs or incremental costs (Quade, 1982, p123).

The picture here is of sunk costs being of no relevance whatsoever to policy-making, and this difference points to a major divergence between the perspectives of the economist and the political scientist. How is it that a political scientist could regard sunk costs as an important determinant of public policy, while economists regard such costs as irrelevancies? Is the difference in perspective simply analogous to the difference between political and economic rationality, or is there a very different problem which must be addressed? This essay explores this grey area of policy studies; it argues that the economists' dictum of 'letting bygones be bygones', of 'not crying over spilt milk' poses very real problems for policy-makers because of the epistemological status of public policies and the consequent nature of the policy process. In so doing it also explores the dynamics of sunk costs over time and points to some important factors relating to the tactics of political advocacy which indicate that sunk costs are not neutral in their impact.

The general theme of the essay relates to the necessity in policy-making to learn from mistakes, contrasted with the injunction (from the economists) to ignore spilt milk and other evidence of mistakes – a point on which economic rationality and a kind of political rationality not covered by Dye (1981) are in agreement rather than in conflict, because political imperatives for hiding the detection of error favour cover-up and lying rather than the honest admission of error. Thus, White Elephants are born. Good policy-making, in contrast, requires policy-makers of the kind for which George Washington was a putative exemplar – who, having felled the cherry tree and been found out, will confess 'I cannot tell a lie . . . .'

Economists and Sunk Costs

Including in one's analysis consideration of 'non-relevant' costs is one of what Robert E. Bickner (1980, p.59) termed 'the pitfalls of analysis':

> Relevant costs are those costs, only those costs, that result from the specific decision or choice being analysed. Any expenditure, for example, or resource commitment or sacrifice, that will occur regardless of the decision being analysed must not be reckoned as a cost of that decision.

And as Bickner (1980, p. 59) went on to point out, 'every primary course in economics dwells on this principle', and economists are at pains to point out the distinctions between fixed costs and variable costs, sunk costs and incremental costs, and recurring costs and non-recurring costs in order to allow a separation of relevant and non-relevant costs. Including sunk costs is even known as the 'sunk costs fallacy'. Despite these careful distinctions and the injunctions of countless economists, there is often a strong temptation to include irrelevant costs, and the economist's meticulous concern for covering costs comprehensively can result in sunk costs or other irrelevant costs being included.

In a footnote, Quade points to the difference between the political and economic perspectives on sunk costs which excited the interest of the present author: 'While sunk costs may be irrelevant as costs, decision-makers are often reluctant to treat them as such. Writing off a cost as sunk may be an admission of failure that could carry political penalties' (Quade, 1982, p123n).

We shall return later to the reasons why policy-makers not only do not ignore sunk costs but regard them as compelling reasons for committing future costs, but for now it should be remarked that the economists should not be let off with such a brief obiter, because the difference between the *prescriptive* advice that sunk costs should be ignored and the *descriptive* remark that people do not ignore them would seem to undermine the economists' view of humanity as utility maximisers. If people act rationally so as to maximise benefits-minus-costs, then why do they act so as to take sunk costs into account rather than ignore them? In considering the case of an individual who ignores the neo-Classical theory of demand and so does not want less of a good when the price rises, Martin Hollis (Hollis, 1977) has pointed out that economists are likely to explain this away by saying that the individual has an indifference map which makes it rational for them to do so, that it is utility that matters, and that the indifference map of some individuals means that their utility is maximised by becoming a monk; if, Hollis adds, the proposition begins to sound tautological 'the only move short of dropping the proposition is to regard it as none the worse for being a tautology' (Hollis, 1977; p182).

But the theory of demand still has considerable value as a theory predicting human behaviour even if it must become tautological in dealing with exceptions; the assumption that people will act so as to maximise utility seems to come entirely unglued when we consider the behaviour of people with regard sunk costs. The answer to this puzzle is, of course, that there are other relevant costs apparent to the policy-maker which make including sunk costs rational behaviour. It is fine, from the point of view of the utility of the individual policy-maker, if these costs are outweighed by the benefits from including sunk costs; where we run into problems is when we consider the utility of the society on whose behalf the policy-maker is acting, because in this case there is no doubt that sunk costs should be ignored. That often they are not is often the source of White Elephants.

There are many areas where the assumptions of rational pursuit of self-interest so dear to the utilitarians and neo-Classical economists run into difficulties. As Jon Elster (1983) has pointed out, one is the area of sour grapes: in his tale, a fox, finding he was unable to take the grapes, adapted his preferences. By deciding to include sunk costs – against the best advice of the economists – the individual decision-maker is similarly adjusting their preferences in a way which is not assumed by neo-Classical theorists. One area of particular concern for students of public policy-making is that of incrementalist approaches to decision-making.

The great strength of Charles Lindblom's (1959) incrementalist approach to decision-making is that it serves not just as a prescriptive model, based upon the marginalist notions of economics, of how we should make decisions, but that it is also a powerful descriptive model which portrays accurately the way in which policy-makers do in fact make decisions. Ignoring the past, decision-makers focus upon changes at the margin. But if sunk costs can be powerful factors in deciding future courses of action, the empirical force of the incremental model is weakened, because we would have to concede that decision-makers are not focusing on marginal adjustments to existing policies because they are behaving in a manner predicted by marginalist theory, but because the inertia of the past, and its representation in politics by those who benefit from existing policies. This makes incrementalism a less glamorous theory and lays it somewhat more bare to those who have always criticised it as being a prescription for inertia, because it strips it of the appealing rationale of describing behaviour predicted by the utilitarian axioms of ignoring the past, and maximising future utility, rather than being a prisoner of it.

One further point about the economists' perspective on sunk costs requires discussion. If we are to ignore past, irrevocable decisions, how are we to learn from our mistakes? The economists do not mean to say, of course, that by not counting sunk costs we should ignore the lessons they represent. We will return to the problems of organisational learning in general a little later, but the point draws attention to a problem: the economists' recommendation to ignore sunk costs reinforces a desire which often exists at a personal level – and which finds ample reinforcement at a social level – to hide one's mistakes.

This points to the fact that sunk costs have an ambiguous place in the political arena: on the one hand, they represent past commitments and therefore reasons for pursuing particular courses of action; on the other hand, they can represent past mistakes which we might wish to remain buried. Both these aspects have a bearing on the issue of veracity in the policy process, since the legacy of the past carries at least some of its force because to deviate from past practice would be tantamount to an admission of past error, in just the same way as some sunk costs resurfacing would highlight error. Kerr (1976) once pointed out that policies have empirical epistemological status (they either work as instruments or they do not), although they might also succeed or fail in terms of normative justification – March and Olsen's (1983) 'logic of consequences' and 'logic of appropriateness' come to mind here.

Good public policy-making requires that we know about and learn from these errors, but such frankness does not always make for good politics. The moral of Parson Weems' fable of young George Washington's rather radical pruning is not about George's honesty, but his father's reaction: harsh reactions to mistakes encourage dishonesty. Oppositional politics is usually rather less kind than was George's father, and so a basic accountability mechanism in politics encourages less than frank disclosure of mistakes, and therefore inhibits policy learning (Howlett, 2012).

Before turning to questions of veracity and learning in the policy process we shall examine some points about the politics of sunk costs.

Political Science and Sunk Costs

In the preceding section we noted that deviating from past decisions would amount to an admission of error. This has consequences for good public policy-making because policy-makers will be reluctant to admit to error, but it should immediately be stressed that there is strong political support from a number of quarters for this tendency to continue past policies. Thomas Dye (1981) covers the reasons concisely.

There may be heavy investments in existing programs ('sunk costs' again) which preclude any really radical change. These investments may be in money, buildings, or other physical items, or they may be in psychological dispositions, administrative practices, prestige or organizational structure. It is accepted wisdom, for example, that organizations tend to persist over time regardless of their utility, that they develop routines that are difficult to alter, and individuals develop a personal stake in the continuation of organizations and practices, which makes radical change very difficult. Hence, not all policy alternatives can be seriously considered, but only those which cause little physical, economic, organizational, and administrative dislocation.

To Dye's (1981) perspective it should be added that the status quo enjoys strong support regardless of the factors he lists which have to do with the psychology of policy-makers and the nature of policy-making institutions. Existing policies also have existing beneficiaries who will, vociferously if need be, defend a policy from any threat of discontinuance (Pierson, 1993 & 2006). Especially when governments are seeking to restrain expenditure generally rather than make explicit choices between existing groups, the beneficiaries of policy termination do not exist as a politically active group and – because the benefits are spread very thinly – are not likely to emerge as a politically active group.

Robert Behn (1981, pp.199-226) developed an illuminating contrast between the concerns of policy analysts and policy politicians. Behn's first contrast concerns the distinction between efficiency and equity. The quest for efficiency, of course, ignores the very distributional issues – who bears the costs and who the enjoys the benefits – that are of such importance to the politician. Some individuals will be worse off under any policy, despite overall efficiency gains, and even if they benefit by the same amount as everyone else. Consider the case of air pollution: an industrialist benefits as much as anyone else from the improvement in air quality resulting from the adoption and implementation of a policy controlling industrial air pollution emissions; but the industrialist must bear the costs of emission control, and might not be able to pass these on to the consumer in full; the industrialist will therefore have a net interest in opposing the policy (and is likely to do so with more vigour than will be shown by the general public in pushing for emission control).

The analyst's concern for efficiency derives at least in part from the fact that there is a single, simple measure of efficiency (net social benefits), while equity can only be described. There is no simple, single measure for determining whether any distribution of income or assets is more equitable than another. The distribution of costs and benefits is less amenable to analysis but is of considerably more interest to the politician. If the costs of a policy are spread widely enough there will be little organised opposition and, if the benefits are narrowly concentrated, there will often be vigorous support for it. These policies are of the type Lowi (1964) termed distributive, and, as Behn notes, abundant examples can be found in the area of water resource development in the United States, where many dams, irrigation schemes and flood control projects were undertaken despite being inefficient according to economic analysis. The (irresistible) underlying political rationality is one we are familiar with:

> The benefits of such projects are . . . quite concentrated (and obvious), while the costs are widely distributed (and unperceived), thus providing some groups with significantly positive net benefits despite the aggregate inefficiency of the projects. Responding then to the views of his most vocal constituents, the politician concludes that the projects are most valuable for them – which indeed they are – and therefore ought to be built. There is no constituency to complain about so dispersed a cost, and that the benefits are obvious while the costs are unperceived further weighs against the analytical perspective. The view of the politician triumphs (Behn, 1981, pp. 204-205).

The economic analyst places the responsibility for ensuring social equity squarely on the shoulders of the politician, but this kind of political rationality does little to foster equity, even though it is driven by distributional concerns. Time frequently becomes an important consideration, with costs displaced onto those in the future who do not vote in the present.

Another important difference between the concerns of analysts and politicians is the way they regard inputs and outputs. It is a fundamental rule of policy analysis that care must be taken to count only the outputs of a public policy in assessing its benefits. Inputs are the costs of the policy, and efficiency is concerned with maximum output per unit input. Behn uses the example of military programs to make the point. The programs of the US Navy, for instance, are to be assessed not on the basis of the number of sailors, ships or missiles, but on the ability of the Navy to carry out particular missions in various locations. The concern for the analyst is how much output (national security) can be obtained by different amounts and mixtures of military expenditure.

> To the politician, however, the benefits of military programs are the inputs (dollars and jobs) and the policy question is how much profit and employment is obtained (by his constituents – don't forget the distribution) for various kinds and levels of military expenditures (Behn, 1981, p. 206).

As Behn pointed out, the lure of comparing policies in terms of their inputs can prove irresistible for politicians. He cited the example of James R. Schlesinger, who stressed the importance (and difficulty) of counting outputs in a scholarly article published in 1968, only to fall into the trap of using input measures almost exclusively when arguing, in 1976, on the basis of inputs that the superpower military balance had swung in favour of the Soviet Union – a perfect example of the aphorism 'where you stand depends on where you sit', because Schlesinger the bureaucrat was doing what Schlesinger the analyst warned against. Of course, if the military is attempting to justify even more defence expenditure, such focusing on inputs without bothering to compare the capabilities of the forces can be very good politics.

It is precisely this difference in perspective between analyst and politician which explains why analysts favour program budgeting, while politicians tend to prefer line-item budgeting: the former focuses on outputs and efficiency, while the latter displays the inputs which the politician identifies as the program benefits.

We can now turn to the difference between the perspectives of the economist or policy analyst and the politician which interests us most here: the way they treat sunk costs. Behn (1981, pp. 211- 212) provides some quotations which typify the thinking of the politician:

> 'It's hard to see why the Defense Department won't move ahead and get a flying aircraft after making such a substantial investment.'

> 'It seems to me that we are diluting the investment that we already have there.'

> 'The problem is, it's there. We must either finish it or leave it as a monument to how bad government can be.

Wildavsky's (1964) classic work *The Politics of the Budgetary Process* is replete with examples of the use of such logic by political actors. This reluctance to admit to previous mistakes forms the basis of a classic budgetary strategy known as the 'foot-in-the-door' or 'camel's nose' (on the basis that, while it might be difficult for a camel to pass through the eye of a needle, it is made easier if one at least starts by getting the narrow part through first).

This strategy involves getting a political commitment to a small initial investment, and then building up on that in subsequent years by arguing that to cancel the project would be a waste of the previous investment. The strategy draws attention to the point that the way in which sunk costs influence the decision-making process is a dynamic one. Once sufficiently far advanced, even the economic analysts will come to support completion of the scheme, because they are concerned only with the remaining costs relative to the remaining benefits. As the project becomes farther advanced, this relationship continues to improve, so that eventually only the last year's costs need to be incurred in order to gain all the benefits originally in prospect. Thus, many uneconomic projects, White Elephants, begin by their proponents driving in the 'thin end of the wedge' or getting 'approval in principle' or approval for a pilot project in the absence of a full, careful evaluation. Political keenness to get projects off the ground before designs have been finalised or properly assessed is a common feature of such projects (Jennings, et al., 2018). It is then argued that it would be a waste not to see the project through to completion. The important thing to note is that the injunction to ignore sunk costs supports the above decision process.

The desire to throw good money after bad in these examples points to a fundamental problem with policy-making: as we saw at the outset, policy-making is a process of learning – the detection and correction of error; policy-makers will, however go to considerable lengths to justify and cover up past mistakes, so that errors will persist, reinforced by the injunction of not worrying about sunk costs.

Psychologically, people often find it hard to abandon chosen courses of action and cut their losses and this is sometimes known as the 'Concorde effect' (Arkes, 1999). There is more discussion of this in the management literature, where the phenomenon of 'escalation of commitment' (Staw, 1976) is often discussed. (See also Sleesman et al., 2012). Although the political science literature does include some criticisms of the economists' view of sunk costs (for example, Nozick, 1993).

In brief, politicians are concerned with sunk costs because they indicate the amount of prestige which has been invested in a project or policy, how much face and credibility they stand to lose if the project is cancelled, so the Concorde program was not stopped even after its folly was apparent (Henderson, 1977). Politicians need to preserve appearances of both being able to exercise correct judgment and being able to achieve results (so that future promises will be believed). Individual consumers are often similarly reluctant to admit (even to themselves) that they have wasted an investment, and the imperative to finish a project will be stronger the larger the size of the investment (in both relative and absolute terms) (Kelly & Milkman, 2013).

Behn (1981, p. 214) attributes these differences in the perspectives of the analyst and the politician to the 'imperative of the constituency' for the politician. Given the limitations on the ability of the market to allocate goods and services in a socially desirable manner, the fact that politicians are responsive to their constituencies should, perhaps, be welcomed, but we have seen here that the pressures exerted on politicians cannot be said to be a reliable reflection of the public interest, because of numerous factors. Time and again projects whose benefits are clearly outweighed by their costs are approved by politicians who are doing nothing more than responding to expressions of preferences from their constituencies. Those preferences for private goods are likely to be overrepresented when compared with those for public goods; many inefficient policies are adopted precisely because of this logic. As Behn (1981, p. 218) puts it, 'economic efficiency itself has no constituency . . .'.

Economists see as one of the strengths of techniques like cost-benefit analysis the fact that the preferences of individuals who are not organised or involved in politics are counted in the demand curves used in the analysis. Economic analysis thus has the potential to limit the vagaries of the political process, even if it does ignore distributive issues. But as Behn (1981, p. 222) pointed out, if policy analysts are to be of much real use, they must not only take account of political feasibility, they must help devise political strategies which will assist the chances of their preferred policies being adopted. The compleat policy analyst will not only recommend the best policy alternative but also the best political strategy with which the client can win the adoption and implementation of this alternative. After all, how can a policy be the 'best' unless it is actually adopted and implemented? In addition, as Formaini (1990) pointed out, cost-benefit analysis can be used only as a tool aiding decision, not as the sole basis for decisions, because it neglects questions of ethics and equity.

Policy-making: Appearances or Substance?

Thus far we have discussed the different perspectives of analysts and politicians in the policy process, and the ways in which these can frustrate our attainment of 'rational' public policy and the avoidance of projects that might become White Elephants. It is now time to remind ourselves that analysts are themselves politicians not neutrals in most cases of public policy-making, and that all participants in the process can have incentives to mislead each other and the public.

Unfortunately, governments and those who serve them distort the truth far too often. Sometimes they tell their citizens downright lies in an effort to cover up mistakes, in an effort to avoid responsibility for them. The muckraker IF Stone maintained that 'Every government is run by liars, and nothing they say should be believed.' It is small wonder, then, that politicians will refuse to ignore sunk costs and will throw good money after bad to avoid the same burden of responsibility. Lying too often (and being found out) can, of course, undermine the credibility of governments; lying in a somewhat trivial area can have broader consequences. Much of the public discourse is, of course, probably better described as 'bullshit' (Frankfurt, 2005), seeking to convey a greater degree of knowledge than one possesses in order to exercise power.

Modern politics frequently involves the creation of image and myth which will strike a responsive chord with the heartstrings of the electorate. This is not just a recent phenomenon. The tales of George Washington's virtues were part of a deliberate attempt to create symbol of unity in the newly established American republic, as was the construction of neoclassical architecture reminiscent of the Roman and Greek republics (Wills, 1984), following the advice of Madison, who had proposed a new form of government, but asked that it be treated as if it were an old one and given the veneration which time bestows on everything.

There is much in the correct packaging of political products which would be regarded as deceptive if it were applied to other products and, in the United States especially, television images can be more decisive than policies in winning campaigns, although as Goodin (1977) pointed out, symbols that provide coherence to a political system are more acceptable than those described by Edelman (1985) that promise, but fail to deliver, effective policies.

If we accept the view that policy-making is, in essence, a process of societal learning, that it involves the detection and correction of error, then the ability of governments to lie, mislead the public and manipulate their perceptions has serious consequences which go beyond questions of morality and to the very core of effective policy-making. Even if we are not interested in ensuring democratic government, with the accountability of policy-makers to the public (which requires that the public knows, with some degree of accuracy, what the government is doing so that they can be praised or blamed for it), effective policy-making requires information which is reliable and accurate. That is to say that even tyrannical government requires good information and good social theory if it is to be effective.

Nevertheless, most autocracies suppress and control information as part of the process of governing without the consent of the governed, but this is usually to their long-term detriment, because if everybody is frightened to criticise policies, to argue over whether they work and bring this information to the attention of the government, mistakes will be perpetuated and policy-making will become farcical because it proceeds on the basis of social theory and data that are about as much use to those steering the 'ship of state' as a map showing the earth as flat. This is why the 'cancel culture' sweeping universities (Flynn, 2020) is particularly hazardous.

The Soviet Union frequently provided examples of the problems of excessive secrecy for governance, despite some obvious advantages. For example, when the disastrous fire at a nuclear power station at Chernobyl released large amounts of radioactive materials into the environment, the Soviets were able to suppress information about the disaster for long enough to ensure an evacuation of thousands of people without panic. In so doing, however, it failed to alert its neighbours over whom much of the radiation spread. (Indeed, the alarm bells were first sounded in Sweden). This secrecy cost it much international goodwill. Another conundrum for the Soviets was AIDS, first identified among homosexuals and spread by unprotected sexual promiscuity involving anonymous partners – both phenomena which were symptoms of 'Western capitalist decadence' and which therefore did not 'officially' exist in the Soviet Union. This official lie caused a dilemma: did the government warn the population and implicitly admit to the past lie (and lose some credibility in the process) or refuse to admit to the problem and sentence many thousands to death at considerable cost via medical care?

The tendency in modern democracies for there to be demands for a move towards 'open government' can be seen, therefore, to have both normative and practical force. The response of governments to these demands has been variable, but many have introduced freedom of information legislation, procedures for public participation and devices to allow citizens cheap and readily available means of questioning the use of administrative discretion. At the same time, the quality of policy-making can be improved, partly because the government bureaucracy does not have a monopoly on information, but partly also because exposing the arguments and evidence underlying any policy to scrutiny and debate can force policy-makers to be careful to get it right before going public with the policy proposal.

Open government is not, of course, without its costs. Opening the policy-making process up to the citizens inevitably improves the access for interest groups and increases political pressures in general. One likely result of this is that the overall level of rationality in the policy process will suffer a further decline as policy-makers are forced to respond more to political forces and less to the force of reason and evidence. There is a danger, therefore, of an accentuation of the already substantial inclination towards the incremental mode of policy-making. Moreover, this increase in political content, while appearing to involve an advancement of democratic norms, will inevitably be open to the tendencies towards special interests and against public interests.

The relationship between responsible, democratic government and 'good' public policy is very complex. In some respects, democratic principles translated into action can be seen to improve the quality of policy-making; in others they constitute a prescription for policy-making which panders to special interests, so that democratic government and rational public policy constitute a dilemma and are unattainable together.

This simply serves to remind us that public policy-making is a highly confused and highly confusing field of enquiry. It is often hard enough to say with any degree of exactitude what the government's policy is in any area, let alone what its goals are, whether they are in the public interest, and whether the policy fulfils them. As we saw in the first section, a policy can mean many things to different people – costs for some; benefits for others; a bigger budget for the implementing agency; 'jobs for the boys' (or girls); tokenism for some; an excessive intrusion of government authority for others.

White Elephants

The kind of decisional logic I have suggested here can also result in the perpetuation of policies or projects that might not withstand scrutiny. One such that I studied was the commitment to construction of the Loy Yang B power station in the Australian state of Victoria (Kellow, 1996). Beset by industrial relations problems dating back to the construction of the Newport station, the government desperately needed to be able to provide continuity of employment for the Loy Yang A station. Problem was, forecast demand could not justify the additional capacity. Enter the Portland Aluminium Smelter, the construction of which was secured by the conclusion of a very generous contract which tied the electricity price to the global price of aluminium.

The construction of desalination plants in five Australian states in the mid-2000s in response to the 'Millennial Drought' also provide good examples of White Elephants, but upon closer examination the cases are complex and varied.

The clearest example is perhaps the Victorian plant near Wonthaggi, costing $3.5b when ordered by the Bracks Labor government in June 2007, with construction completed in December 2012. The drought had broken in 2010 and dam storages returned to normal the year before commissioning, being at 81% of capacity when completed. The plant was immediately mothballed and the first water not produced until March 2017. But this was built as a public-private partnership, and the owners, Aquasure[1], were paid hundreds of millions of dollars for initially delivering no water (Ker, 2014) and even at the time of writing are receiving payment for water delivered when storage dams are 80 percent in advance of what are usually wet months (Johnston, 2021).

The Victorian government decided to proceed with its desalination plant in June 2007 – on average the driest month of the year. This was also the very month that a feasibility study was produced by Melbourne Water and GHD (2007) – not a cost-benefit analysis, but an estimate of costs of various options, with no estimate of benefits. If there was a cost-benefit analysis undertaken, the government did what it could to keep it secret: a citizens group, Your Water Your Say, formed in opposition to the project, sued the government to force release all documentation, but lost, had costs awarded against it, and was forced into bankruptcy by the government.

There was, in short, no slow, careful consideration of the merits of the project, yet the decision represented a complete *volte face*. The Liberal Party had promised a desalination plant before the 2006 state election, but Bracks had criticised the idea. The reason for the change of heart lay probably with the level of alarm generated in the intervening period, especially by the alarmist mammologist Professor Tim Flannery, who was nominated as 'Australian of the Year' in January 2007. Despite lacking credentials in climatology or hydrology, Flannery immediately claimed that 'even the rain that falls isn't actually going to fill our dams and river systems' (Sara, 2007). He followed this up in June, when he said that 'Adelaide, Sydney and Brisbane, water supplies are

---

1   Disclosure: the largest shareholder in Aquasure is UniSuper (Ker, 2016; Thompson *et al.*, 2017), from which the author draws a pension.

so low they need desalinated water urgently, possibly in as little as 18 months' (Flannery, 2007), interestingly omitting Melbourne, even though Bracks announced the project four days after Flannery's editorial in *New Scientist.*

As noted above, political keenness to get projects off the ground before designs have been finalised or properly assessed is a recognised factor in the commission of such errors (Jennings et al., 2018).

Other states did better, realising that water from desalination plants was more expensive than that from dams – an estimated five times the cost in the case of Queensland's Tugun plant. A large part of that cost is marginal or avoidable, and a symposium in Western Australia in which the author participated recommended that the new Kwinana desal plant should be used only on an 'as needed' basis. The take-or-pay contract in Victoria precluded this.

Queensland did better and mothballed its Tugun plant as soon as it was completed because the drought had broken, but subsequent decisions converted the desal plant and a costly water network into embarrassing White Elephants. Despite the drought-causing El Niño being replaced by a rain-inducing La Niña, decision-makers remained drought averse and retained as much water as possible behind Wivenhoe dam, which had been constructed as, *inter alia*, as a means of flood mitigation after the 1974 Brisbane floods.

The very wet summer of 2010-2011 saw the Wivenhoe storage reach 126 per cent of capacity on 13 October, 111 per cent on 21 October, and 123 percent on 29 December. On each occasion, the operator reduced the level to only 100 percent and so when a serious flood began on 11 January 2011 and the storage reached 191 percent, emergency releases were necessary to protect the integrity of the structure, exacerbating the floods downstream (Dragun, 2011). Adherence to past decisions rendered the desalination plant, the water network *and* the flood control dam into White Elephants.

Often, politicians attempt to make a virtue out of their stubbornness. A recent example came from Victorian Premier Daniel Andrews who, confronted with claims that the responses of his government to Covid-19 outbreaks (including lockdowns) were not consistent with the most recent WHO advice (WHO, 2019), stated 'We must stay the course' (ABC, 2020). Staying the course avoids any need to admit error or revisit the original decision.

Sunk costs therefore add momentum to decision processes, psychologically and politically creating momentum towards outcomes selected earlier, good or bad, good investment or White Elephant. Path dependency (David, 1985) is not just a matter of technological choices favouring a continuation of the past, but the capital (not just economic, but psychological and political) already invested in the chosen course of action. A clear example is provided by the decision to use the atomic bomb in 1945. As Isaacson and Thomas (1986) put it, 'A decision to forsake the new $2 billion weapon would be difficult to justify politically, and perhaps even morally.... The process had a momentum of its own...'. The very mechanisms of accountability can limit the admission of errors and thus policy learning because few political actors outside government are as understanding as Washington's father.

The cancellation in September 2021 by the Australian government of the contract to have the French construct diesel submarines in favour of UK and US cooperation to build nuclear powered submarines represents a rare example of sunk costs *not* leading to a number of White Elephants, although this decision was undoubtedly facilitated by the change in prime ministers from Malcolm Turnbull signing the original deal and Scott Morrison breaking it—not to mention only $3 billion of a total cost of $90 billion having been spent.

Conclusion

I have attempted to set out here some often overlooked differences between economic policy analysis and the politics of policy-making that limit veracity and thus learning, making it likely that poor choices will be persisted with rather than abandoned. Sometimes poor choices in a social or economic sense are chosen for political purposes because of the benefits they provide to constituents. As Nikita Kruschev once put it, 'politicians are the same the world over – they promise a bridge even where there is no river.' But the political logic of sunk costs means that there is always a chance a river can be created to prevent having to admit to the initial error. Bad ideas, driven by politics and absent sound policy analysis, can grow into costly White Elephants.

References

ABC News. (2020, August 23). *Daniel Andrews urges Victorians to stay the course in lockdown* (Press release) https://www.abc.net.au/news/2020-08-23/daniel-andrews-urge-victorians-to-stay-the-course/12587178

Arkes, H. R., & Ayton, P. (1999). The sunk cost and Concorde effects: Are humans less rational than lower animals? *Psychological Bulletin, 125*(5), 591–600. https://doi.apa.org/doi/10.1037/0033-2909.125.5.591

Behn, R. D. (1981). Policy analysis and policy politics. *Policy Analysis*, 7(2), 199-226. https://www.jstor.org/stable/42783475

Bickner, R. E. (1980). Pitfalls in the Analysis of Costs. In G. Majone, and E.S. Quade (Eds) *Pitfalls of analysis* (Vol. 8, pp. 57-69). John Wiley & Sons. https://pure.iiasa.ac.at/id/eprint/1228/1/XB-80-108.pdf#page=31

David, P.A. (1985). Clio and the economics of QWERTY. *The American Economic Review* 75: 332-337. https://www.jstor.org/stable/1805621

Downs, A. (1957). *An Economic Theory of Democracy*. Harper & Row.

Dragun, A. (2011, January 9). Far too much water left in the dam. *The Australian.* http://www.theaustralian.com.au/opinion/far-too-much-water-left-in-the-dam/news-story/f26ea537e0fdd09f9bc680240c94 ae62

Dye, T.R. (1981). *Understanding Public Policy* (4th ed.) Prentice-Hall

Edelman, M. J. (1985). *The symbolic uses of politics*. University of Illinois Press.

Elster, J. (1983). Sour Changes: Studies in the Subversion of Rationality. Cambridge University Press.

Flannery, T. (2007). Not such a lucky country. *New Scientist, 194*(2608), 5. https://doi.org/10.1016/S0262-4079(07)61458-4

Flynn, J. R. (2020). *A book too risky to publish: Free speech and universities*. Academica Press.

Formaini, R. L. (1990). *The myth of scientific public policy*. Transaction Books.

Frankfurt, H. (2005). *On Bullshit*, Princeton University Press.

GHD, & Melbourne Water. (2007, June). Seawater Desalination Feasibility Study. June 2007. https://www.water.vic.gov.au/__data/assets/pdf_ file/0026/53864/Feasibility-study_whole-doc.pdf

Goodin, R. E. (1977). Symbolic rewards: Being bought off cheaply. *Political Studies, 25*(3), 383-396. https://doi.org/10.1111%2Fj.1467-9248.1977. tb01287.x

Henderson, P. D. (1977). Two British errors: Their probable size and some possible lessons. *Oxford Economic Papers, 29*(2), 159-205. https:// www.jstor.org/stable/2662657

Hollis, M. (1977). *Models of Man; Philosophical Thought on Social Action*, Cambridge University Press.

Howlett, M. (2012). The lessons of failure: learning and blame avoidance in public policy-making. *International Political Science Review, 33*(5), 539-555. https://doi.org/10.1177%2F0192512112453603

Isaacson, W. & Evan T. (1986). *The Wise Men*, Touchstone.

Jennings, W., Lodge, M., & Ryan, M. (2018). Comparing blunders in government. *European Journal of Political Research, 57*(1), 238-258, 245.

Johnston, M. (2021, April 9). Melbourne dam levels are nearing 80 per cent as $77m worth of desal water keeps pouring in. *Sunday Herald Sun.* https://www.heraldsun.com.au/news/victoria/melbourne-dam-levels-are-nearing-80-per-cent-as-77m-worth-of-desal-water-keeps-pouring-in/news-story/733dc5f2e21486f1ff9853bcecbcfd10

Kellow, A. (1996). *Transforming power: the politics of electricity planning.* Cambridge University Press.

Kelly, T. F., & Milkman, K. L. (2013). Escalation of commitment. In E. H. Kessler (Ed.). (2013). *Encyclopedia of management theory* (pp. 257-259). Sage Publications.

Ker, P. (2014, November 6). Victoria's desalination plant cost taxpayers hundreds of millions of dollars despite delivery of no water. *The Age.* http://www.theage.com.au/victoria/victorias-desalination-plant-cost...ars-despite-delivery-of-no-water-20141106-11hn1y.html#ixzz3IKCcNji5

Ker, P. (2016, March 7). Tertiary education workers biggest winners from Victoria desalination start. *Sydney Morning Herald.* https://www.smh.com.au/business/companies/tertiary-education-workers-biggest-winners-from-victoria-desalination-start-20160307-gncg3u.html

Kerr, D. H. (1976). The logic of 'policy' and successful policies. *Policy Sciences, 7*(3), 351-363. https://doi.org/10.1007/BF00137628

Lindblom, C. E. (1959). The science of "muddling through". *Public administration review, 19*(2), 79-88. https://doi.org/10.2307/973677

Lowi, T. J. (1964). American business, public policy, case-studies, and political theory. *World politics, 16*(4), 677-715. https://doi.org/10.2307/2009452

March, J. G., & Olsen, J. P. (1983, December). 'The new institutionalism: Organizational factors in political life.' *American political science review, 78*(3): 734-749. https://doi.org/10.2307/1961840

Nozick, R. (1993). *The Nature of Rationality.* Princeton University Press.

Olson, M. (1965). *The logic of collective action: Public goods and the theory of groups.* Harvard University Press.

Pierson, P. (1993, July). When effect becomes cause: Policy feedback and political change. *World politics, 45*(4), 595-628. https://doi.org/10.2307/2950710

Pierson, P. (2006). Public policies as institutions. In I. Shapiro, S. Skowronek, & D. Galvin (Eds.). *Rethinking political institutions: the art of the State.* NYU Press.

Quade, E.S. (1982) *Analysis for public decisions.* North Holland.

Sara, S. (2007, February 11). *Interview with Professor Tim Flannery (Television interview).* ABC Landline. https://www.abc.net.au/local/archives/landline/content/2006/s1844398.htm

Simeon, R. (1976). Studying public policy. *Canadian Journal of Political Science/Revue canadienne de science politique, 9*(4): 548-580. doi:10.1017/S000842390004470X

Sleesman, D. J., Conlon, D. E., McNamara, G., & Miles, J. E. (2012). Cleaning up the big muddy: A meta-analytic review of the determinants of escalation of commitment. *Academy of Management Journal, 55*(3), 541-562. https://doi.org/10.5465/amj.2010.0696

Staw, B. M. (1976). Knee-deep in the big muddy: A study of escalating commitment to a chosen course of action. *Organizational behavior and human performance, 16*(1), 27-44. https://doi.org/10.1016/0030-5073(76)90005-2

Thompson, S., Macdonald, A., & Moullakis, J. (2017, December 8). Trickledown economics at UniSuper-backed Aquasure. *Financial Review*. https://www.afr.com/street-talk/trickledown-economics-at-unisuperbacked-aquasure-20171207-h009sa

Weems, M. L. (1962). *The Life of Washington*. M. Cunliffe (Ed.). The Belknap Press of Harvard University Press, 12.

Wildavsky, A. (1964). *The Politics of the Budgetary Process*. Little, Brown and Company

Wills, G. (1984). *Cincinnatus: George Washington and the enlightenment*. Doubleday Books.

World Health Organisation. (2019, September 19). *Non-Pharmaceutical Public Health Measures for Mitigating the Risk and Impact of Epidemic and Pandemic Influenza*. https://www.who.int/publications/i/item/non-pharmaceutical-public-health-measuresfor-mitigating-the-risk-and-impact-of-epidemic-and-pandemic-influenza

CASE STUDY 1

'Water, water everywhere and not a drop to drink"

The sad history of water politics in SE Qld and the bad politics that led to the 'solution' of desalination

Bruce Kingston

Background

Water is often ignored because of its ubiquity but at the same time we humans can maintain life without it for only some 3 or 4 days. Simply put, Australia is a dry continent with limited artesian water, few major rivers and clearly it does not always rain where we need it to. Not surprisingly water policy has been an area of great consternation for successive governments in Australia since the time of the first settlements.

Major dam projects in Australia in the first half of the 20th century were commonly hailed as providing jobs, water security, opening up additional arable land or for other industrial uses and were commonly seen as substantially improving the public good. This era was probably starting to wane in the 1970's as dams such as that proposed on Tasmania's Franklin River became intense political footballs. It was into this political environment that significant discussions were begun to cope with changes afoot in the south east of Queensland.

The Bjelke Petersen government was in the process of creating a business and social environment attractive to intrastate migration and this was driving commercial and residential real estate developments across the south east. New suburbs were springing up, requiring water, power and other related infrastructure. Additionally, in early 1974, devastating floods hit SE Queensland causing loss of life and massive property damage. This, along with the accelerating development of SE Queensland was recognised as a catalyst for the building of a major dam some 80 klm west of Brisbane, Wivenhoe, which would serve not only as water security for the region but also offer some flood mitigation capacity as well. Indeed, its dual role was brought into sharp contrast during arguments regarding liability for flood damage during the 2011 floods in the Brisbane Valley. Wivenhoe was completed in 1984, dramatically increasing the regions water capacity, holding some 1.165 million megalitres at full capacity.

However not long after its completion, a 1988 Cabinet Submission to the Queensland Government from the Queensland Water Resources Commission stated that "the yield of Wivenhoe Dam will be fully committed by about 2015" (Queensland Cabinet Submission 49414, August 1988).

It had also been pointed out that with only one major (and numerous minor ones) dam in the Brisbane River catchment the problems of using Wivenhoe for flood mitigation while maintaining water security for the region was problematic. This issue was highlighted in the reports following the Ipswich and Brisbane floods of 2011 showing the difficult positions of the water supply management roles against those attempting to mitigate floods.

The logical solution to this impending serious problem was the development of another major dam in South East Queensland. A site that had already been identified as an option for a major water catchment for SE Queensland was in the Albert River valley – what was to become known as the Wolfdene Dam. This was considered alongside Wivenhoe in the early 1970's, with Wivenhoe eventually being chosen as it had slightly lower costs, slightly more volume and had the added bonus of flood mitigation on the Brisbane River. A dam of a scale similar to Wivenhoe Dam was projected to solve much of the immediate water issues in the south east until at least 2035. What made this site particularly interesting to water managers was that the proposed site was in an area blessed with consistent and substantial rain. Oddly enough this does not seem to have been a major criterion in the selection of other dam sites since. Wolfdene had particular attraction to those contemplating flood management as it gave the operators of Wivenhoe the opportunity to release water progressively during flood incidents without major consideration of the regions water security. Plans were put in place to commence land acquisitions, with the state commencing these purchases during 1989.

Much of this planning and discussion took place in the tumultuous waning period of the National Party government. Joh Bjelke Petersen had resigned in late 1987 having led the state for 21 years. He was replaced as Premier by Mike Ahern for some 20 months and then Russell Cooper for some 2 months until their loss to the ALP in December 1989. The impending state election of December 1989 saw this crucial piece of infrastructure become a political football.

Add to this the growing environmental movement which had thrown its weight into the Wolfdene debate (and created future political bedfellows) as noted in this Sydney Morning Herald article:

> "As the president of the Australian Conservation Foundation back in 1989, Peter Garrett was a vocal opponent of the Wolffdene Dam proposed for the Gold Coast hinterland. He campaigned alongside aspiring Queensland Labor premier Wayne Goss to stop its construction. The first week after Labor broke the National Party's 30-year stranglehold on Queensland politics, the newly elected Goss government – with Kevin Rudd as its top public servant - canned the Wolffdene Dam. In

years to come, this decision would be labelled short-sighted as south-east Queensland went perilously close to running dry" (Marriner, 2009).

The ALP State Opposition saw the dam as an easy target to gain some environmental credentials and it seems highly likely that they also considered that this issue may swing votes in the outer urban seats north of the gold coast and south of Brisbane where localised opposition to the proposed dam was increasingly vocal. Upon achieving power Premier Goss proceeded to cancel the dam with no other viable alternate programs in place - a decision which would bring water issues into sharp focus as the period of drought conditions came to a head in S E Queensland during the first decade of the 2000's. The 'millennium drought' as it was dubbed saw much of southern and eastern Australia record very low rainfall figures from 1996 until 2010. With no other major infrastructure options available to them, the Queensland ALP government under Premier Wayne Goss and his Chief of Staff Kevin Rudd thought that it could focus on demand management to solve its problems.

Undoubtedly successful as they were in reducing per capita water consumption in the region, increasing population growth as well as industrial requirements for water meant that demand side management could never seriously address the over-arching problem.

Residents of SE Queensland at this time will remember the many advertising programs around water conservation and indeed there was substantial success in reducing demand. However, it seems much of this can only be achieved during periods of emergency. As noted in an industry magazine in recent years:

"South East Queensland sweltered through a hot and dry 2018/19 summer, which saw water use reach its highest levels since the Millennium Drought between 2001 and 2008.

In January, water use across the region peaked at a record 239L per person per day (Lpd), about 25Lpd higher than the same time last year and 70Lpd higher than the average use since the drought" (Butler, 2019).

It is hard to find any academics or resource managers who believe that demand side management can do anything but reduce load on the system in peak periods. It cannot replace the need for greater water capacities to cope with rapidly growing communities across the region.

In 2011 the Council of Mayors (representing all 11 major Councils in SE Queensland and approximately 1/6th of Australia's population) made a scathing response to the Productivity Commission's Public Inquiry into Australia's Urban Water Sector.

"In 2007, South East Queensland earned the distinction of becoming one of the first major metropolitan regions in the world to almost run out of water. With $7 billion of borrowed State funds later, we have now earned the reputation as having some of the most expensive white elephants in water infrastructure in Australia, with a $2.5 billion recycling system the Government had pledged not to turn on until dams are below 40 per cent, a $1.2 billion desalination plant that won't be turned on until dams are below 60 per cent, and a pipeline to a dam the State never built - but spent $265m in non-recoverable costs in not doing it" (Productivity Commission, 2011).

Large volumes of public money were put into water conservation measures and while household use was able to be substantially reduced, the government were still being warned of the very real possibility of the south east of the state actually having insufficient water to meet household and industrial needs. It was in this environment that the option of desalination was grasped as a quick fix.

While there are obviously numerous options for studying

white elephants in this subject area, I have chosen to focus on the Gold Coast Desalination Plant (GCDP) for this chapter. It has all the hallmarks of a classic government white elephant:

- very expensive to construct at some $1.2 billion dollars,
- very expensive to operate using large amounts of electricity,
- producing water at some 6 time the cost per kilolitre of conventional dams,
- having some significant environmental concerns, and
- not really addressing the problem in the longer term with a limited functional lifespan.

So what is desalination?

Desalination has been around for thousands of years. Greek sailors used to boil water and collect the vapour to augment their freshwater supplies on long journeys. Modern desalination was invented in the 1950's in the US and nuclear powered desal plants producing vast quantities of water were proposed shortly after though these never came to fruition. It was also considered in the 1950's in Australia.

The most common form of desalination nowadays involves the pumping of sea water at very high pressure through synthetic membranes to remove salt and other impurities in a process known as reverse osmosis. There are some 16,000 major desalination plants worldwide across 177 countries, though they are most common in extremely dry areas such as the middle east and on islands with limited water capacities. Desalination is a highly energy intensive process, consuming some 2.5-3.5 kwh of electricity for every thousand litres of fresh water produced. Of course operating in this saline environment means that corrosion becomes a significant problem, something which was to plague the GCDP in its early years. Desal plants can also have significant environmental impacts. The brine (and chemicals used in the filtration process) which is removed from the sea water is pumped back into the ocean with high levels of salt and impurities reintroduced into the sea potentially causing areas of hypersalinity. Additionally, the pumping and infrastructure associated with the plants have had significant impacts on sealife.

Therefore, along with the very high costs of the physical plant construction and high costs of water produced we need to also factor in the high energy costs and environmental impacts when assessing the virtues of desalination as a viable option for meeting the water needs of a region.

What was the GCDP?

The GCDP is a 'two-pass' reverse osmosis desalination plant. The first pass removes salt, minerals and other microscopic particles, while the second pass targets boron and bromide specifications suitable for drinking water.

As well as the core desalination equipment, the GCDP includes a 1.5 kilometre marine intake and outlet tunnels, a 25 kilometre pipeline to connect to the South East Queensland Water Grid at Worongary, a pump station and a small reservoir.

The Gold Coast City Council initially developed plans for a smaller 55 megalitre per day desalination plant with a projected cost of some $260 million. With the worsening drought conditions in South East Queensland, the state government joined the project and expanded the projected water production to 133 megalitres per day with the state government contributing an additional $869 million to the project.

Somewhat counterintuitively, this equates to a 430%increase in cost for 240% increase in capacity.

The Gold Coast Desalination Alliance was formed by a consortium of five companies – Cardno, Sinclair Knight Merz, Veolia Water and John Holland Group and proceeded to select the Bilinga site near the Gold Coast airport as the most suitable location for construction.

Over a period of approximately 2 and a half years from August 2006, the project moved from design, to construction to commissioning, producing the first water supply to the grid in February 2009.

In July 2009, a report sent to the State Government identified 16 substantial issues requiring rectification. These included minor cracking in the intake and outlet shaft of the plant, incorrect water pressure pumps having been used in parts of the plant, lower-grade steel was used in places throughout the plant and corrosion to 26 non-return valves because of manufacturing errors. Rectification of these and other issues delayed handover of the plant to the government. Significant rust issues delayed the opening of the plant and continued to plague the plant. The GCDP was officially handed over the state government in October 2010.

Almost immediately after opening, water storages for SE Queensland rose to more than 60% capacity and by late 2010 had reached an effective 100% capacity. In December 2010 the state government confirmed that the plant would go into standby mode as a cost saving measure.

The GCDP has briefly returned to service on a number of occasions to augment water grid supplies but is primarily operated in standby mode.

What were the adverse effects?

According to the Minister for Natural Resources, Mines and Energy in response to a May 2018 Question on Notice in the Queensland Parliament the cost of producing a megalitre of water from the GCDP was approximately $800. This contrasted markedly with the average cost from traditional dam supplies at approximately $123 per megalitre, or 650% of the cost of dam supplied water.

"The Australia's Urban Water Sector inquiry, conducted by the Australian Government's Productivity Commission in 2011, estimated that the operating costs of desalination plants in Australia were likely to vary from about $500 per megalitre to $1 100 per megalitre. Based on Seqwater's projections, if the GCDP operated at full capacity, it would fall within the higher end of this range at $1 021 per megalitre. However, when production is below full capacity, as is currently the case, the plant's running costs are significantly higher than this benchmark. For example, in 2011–12, operating and maintenance costs were $4 403 per megalitre or approximately four times higher than the maximum estimated by the inquiry" (Queensland Audit Office, 2012-13).

Though not expressly detailed in government papers, the higher cost of producing water from the GCDP must increase the water costs of SE Queensland residents.

Additionally, each kilolitre of water produced expends some 3.6 kilowatt hours of electricity. The GCDP is at pains to explain that it carbon offsets some proportion of this but given the reality of Queensland's reliance in the near term on coal fired power stations, this really only amounts to some form of 'greenwashing'. By choosing to spend funds on carbon offsetting they are simply further increasing the real costs of their per litre production.

The lifecycle cost of the project needs also to be considered as major international studies have suggested the likely economic lifespan of major desalination plants is in the order of 20 - 25 years. With the GCDP now in the second year of its second decade, its useful lifespan may only be until the early 2030's. This offers another substantial issue for consideration. What will be done to ensure the water security of SE Queensland in the coming decades?

Had the Wolfdene Dam been built as planned during the 1990's, the projected costs were estimated to be in the order of $900 million - $1 billion and the likelihood of the impacts of the millennium drought would have been substantially reduced. It should also be remembered that dams commonly have a substantial lifespan (50 years +) and as such would have been producing potable water for the region well into this millennium with minimal additional capital outlay and at a dramatically reduced operating costs.

Could it have been avoided and/or made better

Consistent expert advice both from with and without government over decades has clearly indicated that substantial additional water storage for SE Queensland in particular (but including other major regional centres as well) was not only prudent but absolutely necessary. Even today, there are few experts that believe that the water requirements of this growth can be managed predominantly through demand management. Recycled water use is sometime touted as an option to relieve some pressure on the water grid, however successive governments and levels of government that have embraced this option have quickly sought out other more attractive policies when community distaste for this option rears its head.

Even as late as 2004, an SEQ Water strategy document did not raise the alarm regarding the state of the water problem in the south east. The Queensland Audit Office (QAO) stated:

> "This report was prepared with limited demand data and applied inconsistent methodologies in determining supply availability…. The 2004 strategy did not consider a drought scenario to stress test the water supply arrangements. The emergency water supply situation developed without any contingency planning or prepared solutions available to government to address the emerging critical supply shortage from a severe and prolonged drought (Queensland Audit Office, 2012-13).

The Audit Office went on to note a further SEQ Water strategy document appeared a year later stating

> "In September 2005, a new strategy was released, titled Responding to Drought in SEQ-Contingency Planning for Urban Water Supplies, which addressed the ongoing drought and diminishing water supply levels. This report presented a scenario that water supplies may run out in less than three years, giving limited time to find additional climate-resilient water supplies. Desalination plants in Adelaide and Perth each involved an approval and construction phase of four years, extended to at least five years when the planning and procurement phases were included. In comparison, the delivery time frames for the GCDP and WCRWS were very aggressive and compressed (Queensland Audit Office, 2012-13).

Perhaps even more damningly, the QAO went on to state,

> "Robust program and budget management was not evident at the preliminary decision making stages, as evidenced by the significant discrepancy between initial estimates of construction costs and the forecast target outturn cost/target operating cost determined jointly by the alliance partners (Queensland Audit Office, 2012-13)."

One of the key findings of the QAO was that there was no robust business case for the GCDP. The went on to point out that:

> "All costs have significantly exceeded initial expectations, adversely affecting the value for money proposition for these assets. Rushed planning, and the procurement method chosen to deliver them, meant that achievement of lowest or 'least cost' outcomes cannot be demonstrated (Queensland Audit Office, 2012-13).

In taking over the Gold Coast City Council's (GCCC) 55 megalitre desalination program with a projected cost of some $160 million and doubling its output, the initial assessment by the GCCC team was $265 million. However, within 6 months, and following a fast-tracked contractor selection process, this figure rose dramatically to a projected $869 million and an eventual figure of some $1.2 billion.

This knee-jerk planning and the obvious need to 'do something' in the face of increasing community unrest saw normal procurement procedures drastically curtailed and many of the normal approached to major capital investments almost missing entirely.

This led the QAO to state in 2012 that,

> "For the GCDP in particular, it is not possible to determine with sufficient reliability whether the plant was constructed at best cost, or is being operated and maintained efficiently since. This is because it did not have a formally documented business case; a non-price competitive procurement strategy was chosen to deliver it; and it has not operated to its design capacity, or consistently in any one mode, since its commissioning " (Queensland Audit Office, 2012-13).

To be kind, this suggests a far from strategic approach by the government of the day to such a crucial issue as water security but one which becomes understandable in the more 'executive' focused government which had emerged since the public sector management changes of the Goss/Rudd era. With more centralised decision-making and a much more politicised senior public service working on renewable contracts, and a constant focus on short term news cycles and polling, strategic government planning has been seriously diminished and the more difficult decisions involving major capital works too easy to leave to another government in a few years.

However, what you couldn't ignore is that growth projections for SE Queensland have largely and consistently been proved to be very much on the pessimistic side. Even today in the third year (2022) of the Covid pandemic there are indications that, if anything, intrastate migration has been increasing, putting even greater strain on the region's infrastructure. There are few indications or pundits which suggest that this trend will not be a long term issue for the Queensland Government to deal with.

The Queensland Government's own peak water agency for the region, SEQ Water, in its web document "Planning your water future" states:

> Currently South East Queensland uses around 300,000 million litres a year. By 2046, with our increasing population, the forecast medium demand is around 525,000 million litres a year. With all South East Queensland water grid assets available and operating (including the Western Corridor Recycled Water Scheme), our region's bulk water system can supply about 440,000 million litres a year. Our bulk water supply system meets our region's current needs but in the future new sources will be required to meet the needs of our growing population, expected to reach 5.1 million by 2046 (SEQ Water, 2018).

This is part of a colourful and friendly ebrochure about saving water and looking after the environment, but one cannot ignore their own statistics. Simply put, this means that the water grid (N.B. using recycled water as well) will be some 85,000 million litres short within 25 years. One wonders what happens to these calculations should another millennium drought occurs?

Additionally, it had been established that additional large scale water storage apart from Wivenhoe Dam would allow Wivenhoe to fulfill one of its original and important roles as part of the regions flood mitigation programs. This issue seems to have been completely overlooked in the development of the desalination program.

It is somewhat disingenuous to claim that the desalination plant now plays an integral part of the SE Queensland water security program as this security only comes at a vastly increased cost per kilolitre of water produced and represents only at best a relatively short-term fix to an overwhelming problem.

The GCDP was commissioned when Queensland was working hard to live up to its self-appointed moniker "The Smart State" and as such perhaps too much reliance was placed on the high-tech nature of this 'solution'.

At the risk of seemingly over-simplistic, the major option that suggests itself would be to follow the advice of experts in the first place and build a dam where it actually rains. A significant issue facing any water managers nowadays is the virtual impossibility of building major dams in any locations near major population centres. Between NIMBY voters and environmental protestors, most governments seem to see dam construction as a bridge too far (to mix my infrastructure metaphors).

Perhaps it's time for a government serious about tackling issues like this to bite the bullet and make water security a key plank in their election platform.

References

Butler, L. (2019, May). Managing water demand in South East Queensland. *Utility.* https://utilitymagazine.com.au/managing-water-demand-in-south-east-queensland/

Marriner, C. (2009, November 17). Dam Busters. *Sydney Morning Herald.* https://www.smh.com.au/environment/dam-busters-20091116-iiao.html

Productivity Commission. (June 2011). *Submission to the Productivity Commission's Public Inquiry into the Australian Urban Water Sector.* https://www.pc.gov.au/inquiries/completed/urban-water/submissions/subdr159.pdf

Queensland Audit Office. (2012-13). *Report 14 : Maintenance of Water Infrastructure Assets.* https://www.qao.qld.gov.au/sites/default/files/reports/rtp_maintenance_of_water_infrastructure_assets.pdf Qld Cabinet Submission 49414. (August 1988). Queensland Water Resources Commission – Wolfdene Dam – Value to Brisbane and Costs to the Community. https://www.archivessearch.qld.gov.au/api/download_file/DR47138

SEQ Water. (2018). *Planning for your water future.* https://www.seqwater.com.au/sites/default/files/2019-11/Brochure%20-%20Realities%20of%20Rain%20-%20Planning%20your%20water%20future%20-%20Sunshine%20Coast.pdf

CASE STUDY 2

Murray-Darling Basin Water Reforms – Money for Nothing and Water for Free

Nadeem Samnakay

Introduction

In this essay, the Commonwealth government's 2007 Murray-Darling Basin (MDB) water reforms are critiqued as an example of a 'white elephant' environmental policy. Over $13 billion of Commonwealth funds have been allocated to developing and implementing the reforms, with considerable opacity about the environmental gains and of what $6 billion of expenditure on irrigation infrastructure has achieved in the public interest.

The reforms were really a centralising of water governance arrangements to the Commonwealth and represent a restructuring of governance arrangements, rather than a deliberate attempt at delivering environmental outcomes. Typically, environmental policy reforms require a contraction of natural resource use, achieved for example by industry exit packages and adjustment incentives. The opposite has occurred in MDB water reforms wherein the industry has expanded and obtained more water, and the environment has lost water (Wentworth Group, 2020. Wheeler *et al.*, 2020. Williams & Grafton, 2019.).

The publicly funded irrigation efficiency programs have concentrated wealth to the private sector. They have also legitimised previously unpermitted use of water through granting of entitlements in the case of floodplain water diversions. The centralisation of governance has at best, resulted in the expansion of some environmental initiatives, the basis of which were already agreed upon through pre-existing arrangements with State (including Territory) governments. There was no need for a Commonwealth power grab – one which has become an enormously large bureaucratic labyrinth lacking transparency in how public funds have been spent.

Why chosen – what makes this case study a 'white elephant'?

Determining costs and benefits of an environmental outcome can be challenging because the benefits are not readily amenable to economic quantification. There are methodologies which aim to quantify in dollar terms the benefits we derive from improved environmental condition, but in the main, we value the environment for more than its monetary value. A valuation of the benefits of the MDB Basin Plan has been published (CSIRO, 2012), but only accentuates the subjectivity in monetising environmental benefits.

The MDB water reforms discussed here commenced with Prime Minister John Howard's National Plan for Water Security (NPWS) which was accompanied by the passage of the Commonwealth *Water Act 2007* (the Act). The Act has empowered the Commonwealth government to spend in excess of $13 billion in the MDB. The water shortages arising from the 1997 - 2010 Millennium Drought, which manifested in significant declines in environmental flows in the Basin, served as a policy driver for the NPWS. With over a century of river regulation (i.e., infrastructure projects to support irrigation developments) in the MDB, too much water has been allocated for irrigated agriculture as a consumptive use of water, with the environment bearing the burden of insufficient freshwater flows. The Act has a primary objective of addressing this problem of over allocation.

The NPWS outlined a ten-point plan, to expend $10 billion over ten years. A little too convenient for a document which claims to be well costed (The Age, 2007). The NPWS sought, amongst other things, to "address once and for all water over-allocation in the Murray-Darling Basin" (Howard, 2007). A problem which Howard emphasised was created by the States. While absolutely correct in this summation, blaming your counterparts when you need their help in achieving your outcomes is deeply counterproductive.

Dilemmas in federation and the Australian Constitution

The States, in agreeing to Federate in 1901, retained their powers in managing natural resources when framing Australia's Constitution. Essentially, the legal responsibility for managing water and other natural resources rests with the States. The Commonwealth government has no authority to tell the States what to do in a legislative sense. The Commonwealth's most effective lever for influencing natural resource outcomes is by coordinating and funding national programs from the large amounts of taxation revenue it raises.

Howard, as Prime Minister, sought greater authority in water management and through the Act created the Murray-Darling Basin Authority (MDBA) to lead the water reforms. He had wanted the States to cede their constitutional powers over water to the Commonwealth, but they didn't.

The Act was subsequently passed as a result of the Commonwealth's international affairs powers, in the main relating to international agreements such as the Ramsar Convention on Wetlands and numerous bilateral migratory bird agreements relating to those species which migrate seasonally between wetlands in Australia and northern hemisphere habitats. The absence of constitutional powers being ceded to the Commonwealth means that the Murray-Daring Basin Authority, to put it bluntly, lacks authority. There are no compliance or enforcement measures which can be effectively applied to hold States to account. Implementing the Act still requires cooperation with States – with all the political problems this entails (see Painter,1996) – just as it was prior to centralisation.

Under Howard's original concept of NPWS implementation, of the $10 billion budgeted, $6 billion was to be expended on modernising on and off-farm irrigation infrastructure, and up to $3 billion was to address over-allocation of water in the MDB through buybacks of entitlement as a secondary initiative. Given that over-allocation was the primary policy problem to be solved, it is legitimate to ask why the minor share of the "detailed and costed" budget was for solving over-allocation directly, and the greater share of the budget went to subsidising private wealth maximisation?

At the higher level, the attributes that frame the NPWS as a white elephant are:

- Costs exceed benefits given that large amounts of public funds were given to private enterprises for improving irrigation efficiency, with little to show as environmental outcomes, or for the public good outcomes.
- The causes and remedies of environmental problems are plagued by value judgements yet the Act is dismissive of this requiring that the Basin Plan be based on the 'best available scientific knowledge'.

- The impact and effectiveness of irrigation efficiency projects for recovering environmental water is ambiguous. The overall expenditure of $6 billion lacks transparency with questionable benefits for the 'national interest', especially when compared to using those funds for other nation building programs.
- Policy implementation has been subjected to an inordinately enormous contest of political dualling, both within State and Commonwealth spheres and between political parties. No one can agree on what the desired objectives really are, or for that matter what the problem is, while the States hold power to do as they wish.
- The small gains from policy implementation to date could have been achieved without centralisation and with considerably less Commonwealth investments, using tied grants and incentive-based payments.
- The policy course should change but cannot be undone. 'Staying the course' is the Commonwealth mantra and the appetite for further changes to water governance are very low, politically and amongst MDB irrigation communities. But change will be inevitable.

These matters will be elaborated on below.

What happened?

Within a few months of announcing the NPWS plan, the Rudd Labor government came into power and added a further $3 billion to water reforms through the Water for the Future National Partnership Agreement (NPA). The policy fiascos and failures of this entire $13 billion water reform journey are not reiterated here, but the findings of the Murray-Darling Basin Royal Commission (South Australia, 2019) provide many insights of failures relating to MDB water initiatives (see Beasley, 2021).

Under the Act, the primary task of the MDBA was to develop the Basin Plan, which amongst other tasks, was required to determine a Sustainable Diversion Limit (SDL). Essentially, the MDBA was mandated to define, using "best available scientific knowledge", a limit (a cap) on how much water could be extracted from MDB surface and groundwater sources. The SDL had to reflect an environmentally sustainable level of take (ESLT).

This process of defining an SDL served to energise the politics and pitted conservationists against irrigation interests. Irrigators claimed that regional communities would be devastated by returning some water back for environmental purposes, and conservationists wanted significant volumes of water to be re-allocated for environmental outcomes. The MDBA determined that, on average, something in the order of 3000 to 8000 gigalitres (GL) of water would need to be returned to the environment on an annual basis to achieve an ESLT. The higher the recovery volume, the greater the certainty of environmental outcomes.

After some quite heated rural politics, in 2012, the Basin governments agreed to the Basin Plan. The politically agreed decision required that the Commonwealth would recover from the consumptive pool, only 2750 GL of water, to be returned to the environment to address the problem of over allocation. Under the Rudd government, most of this recovery was going to be achieved by buying water entitlements from irrigators willing to sell some or all of their entitlements. A contrast to Howard's original plan of preferencing irrigation infrastructure upgrades.

The Rudd government supported much of the intent of the NPWS with one other major change. The original intention under Howard's plan was to retain the Murray-Darling Basin Commission (MDBC) and introduce a new Commonwealth agency, the MDBA, specifically to develop and oversee the implementation of the Basin Plan. The Rudd government was not in favour of two separate entities and in 2008 the

MDBC was abolished and transitioned to the MDBA as a Commonwealth agency – albeit with many existing functions still accountable to the Basin States.

MDBC achievements in cooperative federalism

The MDBC was a non-government entity funded collectively by Basin governments[2] responsible for administering the Murray-Darling Basin Agreement. It was accountable to all Basin governments. Its decision making was consensus-based and over time it developed and managed a portfolio of environmental and water programs jointly agreed to by Basin governments, with the Commonwealth as a contributing partner. It was a model of cooperative federalism. The MDBC was often criticised for an overly slow and cumbersome approach to getting consensus agreements on where pooled funds should be spent. It wasn't known for driving transformative change, but its programs generally endured once established.

One of its key achievements was establishing a limit on further water extractions, referred to as a 'Cap'. The Cap limited water extractions to 1993/94 levels of development and was seen as "... an essential first step in establishing management systems to achieve healthy rivers and sustainable consumptive uses...". The States had agreed to being held to account through a compliance audit which was made transparent through public reporting mechanisms. The Cap was a moratorium on any additional extractions of surface water in the Basin "... while the precise details of the Cap on future diversions and its implementation are established (MDBMC, 1996)". The MDBA was meant to continue auditing the Cap under the

---

2   Basin governments of the Murray-Darling Basin Commission include all the jurisdictions which have the Murray-Darling Basin within their boundaries. These include New South Wales, Queensland, Victoria, South Australia and the Australian Capital Territory. The Commonwealth government was also a contributing member.

Water Act but didn't.

By 2007, the States had not made any further efforts to limit extractions, including on groundwater, which the Basin Plan has achieved. However, the mechanism for doing so already existed, it just needed incentivising. The Commonwealth government could have provided this incentive without expending the greater share of $13 billion. The States are receptive to receiving Commonwealth funds and the Commonwealth has a precedence for managing grants tied to performance outcomes without centralising power.

In addition to the Cap, in 2004, Basin governments (excluding Queensland as it does not sit in the catchment of the Murray River) had agreed to the Intergovernmental Agreement on Addressing Over-allocation and Achieving Environmental Objectives in the Murray–Darling Basin. Known as The Living Murray (TLM) program, it formalised a 'First Step' towards recovering water for the environment. TLM came with a commitment of $500 million to recover 500GL of water for managing six iconic floodplain wetlands and $150 million for water management structures to facilitate delivery of that environmental water (MDBA, 2011). This process occurred without centralisation of governance arrangements, nor large subsidies paid to irrigators.

Going purely by the numbers, a cooperative model expended $500 million to get 500 GL back to the environment in four years. The Commonwealth expended over $10 billion to achieving a 2750GL target over thirteen years. It is difficult to see how this amounts to value for money for public expenditure when compared to what a cooperative model of Basin management had achieved.

Why it went wrong?

Putting aside the question of whether the new federally administered governance measures are an improvement or not, implementation of the Basin Plan, which was gazetted in 2012, took a significant change in course in 2013 with Tony Abbott as Prime Minister. The Abbott government was clearly not a supporter of environmental policies, nor of specialised federal agencies responsible for implementation and oversight. Small government was good government.

National Water Initiative outlined a framework for water reform

The National Water Commission (NWC), established in 2004 to oversee national water reforms was one of the agencies promptly abolished by the Abbott government. The NWC had a key function of reporting on compliance by the States on progress towards implementing objectives of the Intergovernmental Agreement on a National Water Initiative (NWI). One of the objectives of the NWI, which all the States had signed onto, was to "return overallocated or overused systems to environmentally sustainable levels of extraction" (COAG, 2004). The very thing the *Water Act 2007* required, but some three years after all Australian States had already signed on to in a cooperative approach to managing the national interest.

The Water Act in 2007 assigned the NWC to report on the effectiveness of Basin Plan implementation – an evaluation function that one would ordinarily deem important for an investment of over $10 billion dollars. On abolishing the NWC, this responsibility transferred to the Productivity Commission which lacks the holistic water governance specialisation of the NWC. An expert-based independent performance evaluator was decommissioned.

The MDBA was also earmarked for dismantling under the Abbott government, but survived. The reason for this is unclear, though it was speculated that functions such as managing water delivery in the highly regulated River Murray necessitates intergovernmental arrangements, irrespective of ideological biases favouring small government. It may have been too difficult or too embarrassing to re-establish the MDBC after the Commonwealth government so eagerly wanted to take control of MDB water governance.

The subtle art of governing in a federation

After decades of working in a federation, the States have learnt a thing or two about 'cost shifting'. Cost shifting is where the States have the Constitutional responsibility to fund and manage programs from their own revenue sources but transfer this expense to the Commonwealth through the delicate art of brokering deals. A federal desire to take over the MDBC provided the ideal opportunity for the States to wash their hands of any funding commitments. By the time the Abbott government took power, the States had withdrawn from funding most of the environmental programs they had previously cooperated on.

Some notable MDBC programs abolished after the formation of the MDBA, or where States withdrew their contributions from, included:

- Cap compliance as noted above.
- Sustainable Rivers Audit – a comprehensive program of monitoring ecological health of Basin rivers. There is no Basin-wide ecological health monitoring program now.
- Risks to Basin Water Resources program – a program which aimed to better understand the risks to water resources, including

climate change (which the MDBA was meant to factor into their setting of SDLs but didn't).

- The Native Fish Strategy – A community-based program of improving fish habitat and fish recovery. After the 2018/19 drought which resulted in sizeable populations of fish dying through declines in water quality, the Commonwealth government is now funding a science program which includes native fish recovery.

- The South East Australia Climate Initiative – a major cooperative climate research program designed to understand rainfall and moisture profiles in catchments, which are being disrupted by climate change.

So, the States withdrew their funds and handed over responsibilities to the Commonwealth. The Commonwealth, not having powers or resources to implement programs has established new working arrangements with the States, which are not dissimilar to how the MDBC functioned – by various joint government committees. Progress is slow, consensus views are still necessary in the main, and the States have the detailed knowledge and the authority.

New South Wales, which has the greatest share of Basin real-estate, has been happily gaming the federal system to their advantage. They are soon to issue water rights to floodplain harvesters for free. These are irrigation enterprises in the upper Darling River system who have been harvesting overland flows and storing these in large dams. This widespread activity represents large volumes of unmetered water extractions, that goes against the spirit of limiting extractions under the Plan and the Cap. These extractions change river flows and distort the analysis of an SDL.

The Commonwealth government, thanks in large part to the Australian Broadcasting Commission's investigative program, Four Corners (Besser, 2017, July 24), has accepted that compliance is an important function when expending public funds. Following a recommendation from the Productivity Commission, it has separated the compliance functions which the MDBA was meant to be responsible for administering and created a new entity. The Inspector-General of Water Compliance now overseas this function supported by the Office of Water Compliance.

A critical element of Basin Plan implementation, and thus compliance, is the development of Water Resource Plans (WRPs). A WRP provides the detail of how water is to be managed in each sub-catchment of the MDB and how the SDL will be adhered to. Under the Water Act all WRPs were meant to be accredited by the MDBA by 2019. As of 2021, New South Wales has had most of its WRPs withdrawn on account that they do not meet the requirements of the Basin Plan, and the State is in no hurry to deliver compliant plans. The States are not only good at cost shifting, they are also very good at gaming the Commonwealth and their counterpart States.

There is essentially nothing the Commonwealth can do to hold NSW or other States to account as it has no constitutional powers to do so. Noting that small government is good government, there are now four Commonwealth agencies managing a bureaucratically burdensome water governance program, comprising of:

- The Department of Agriculture, Water and the Environment
- The Commonwealth Environmental Water Holder and its Office
- The Inspector General of Water Compliance and its Office; and
- The Murray Darling Basin Authority.

This does not include the Productivity Commission responsible for reporting on the effectiveness of implementation. Small government has its limits once the public begins to expect good performance from its taxes.

Capturing rural votes when in coalition

Managing water as a resource is, and always will be political. As an essential element of life, it affects each and every one of us, so we all have a vested interest in how it is managed, even if we earn no income from its consumption. It also affects the quality of the environment in which we live. Indeed some earn their livelihoods from the presence of a healthy river system without consuming water, such as tourism operators and floodplain graziers. Then there are those who have rights to its consumptive use for commercial gain, like irrigators. Some irrigation enterprises earn large profits from having access to water rights and they have lobbying power. In the Murray-Darling Basin, these lobbyists have succeeded in having the taxpayer subsidise their ability to generate large profits with no oversight. The environmental costs have been socialised and the benefits have been privatised. It is a stretch to see how the national interest is being served.

Recalling that the Rudd government gave preference to expending the $3 billion on purchasing water entitlements as a priority in preference to subsiding infrastructure upgrades. This as it turns out is the most cost-effective way to recover water entitlements and solve the problems of over allocation.

It is difficult to see where the public good outcomes are from subsidising irrigation over other uses for that money – unless we accept the principle of trickle-down economics. There was no market failure of the irrigation sector – the market failure was and is under-pricing the environment. So why then would a conservative government, which upholds the market as the preferred way of allocating resources, subsidise the irrigation sector to the tune of $6 billion. The irrigation sector was making profits on aggregate but received windfall government assistance. At the same time, the Australian car manufacturing industry, supposedly generating enormous downstream economic activity, had to fend for itself and collapsed.

Are rural industries a special case? Perhaps the answer lies in the politics of regions and what Botterill (2016) eloquently terms 'agrarian-sentiment'? Tilling the land is part of our heritage. Or perhaps it is to maintain the delicate inconvenient marriage that forms the Liberal-National party coalition? Or perhaps it's okay in a healthy democracy for lobbyists to determine what is in the national interest?

The National Party's Barnaby Joyce, in charge of the water portfolio in the Abbott government, made it abundantly clear that the national interest was not served by protecting "frogs" (Bettles, 2020). He promptly halted the policy of purchasing water entitlements from willing sellers, and prioritised infrastructure upgrades as a means of recovering water. By 2015, the Commonwealth government had purchased 1500 GL of water entitlements towards the SDL target of 2750 GL. The balance was to be obtained through water efficiency gains. The argument goes that by limiting wastage of water in irrigation schemes, 50% of those water savings would return to the environment, and 50% will be retained by the irrigation industry. Irrigators got more water, not less, and for free.

The cost inefficiency of irrigation infrastructure upgrades as a means of recovering water has been analysed by various economists. For example, Loch *et al.* (2014) find that purchasing water entitlements cost the Commonwealth government on average $1450 per megalitre (ML), whereas infrastructure-based recovery costs between $2340 to $5109 per ML as a conservative estimate. Quiggin (2012) surmises that spending the entire $10 billion on water entitlement recovery would yield upwards of 5000GL of water. Returning 5000GL to the environment would give a higher certainty of improved ecological health as scientifically determined by the MDBAs preliminary assessments of what constitutes an environmentally sustainable level of take (MDBA, 2010).

The argument promoted by Joyce and lobbyists is that regional communities will be decimated by removing water from 'productive use'. This is essentially saying that water use for irrigation is more important than water for other values. More important than basic human needs as was evidenced by mostly Indigenous communities along the Darling river in the 2018-19 drought.

Supposedly, by providing subsides for irrigation infrastructure, irrigation dependent communities will prosper, which is good for regional economies. Three fallacies (at least) arise from this logic. Firstly, irrigation infrastructure expenditure is not the best way to achieve the goal of regional development (Wittwer & Dixon, 2013). If you want regions to prosper, invest wisely in public assets. These could be things like schools, universities, hospitals or such, that could easily be funded in a budget of $6 billion.

The second is that it assumes that profits from irrigation enterprises are largely spent in the regions where irrigation takes place. The community conscious irrigator will not spend their profits buying luxury coastal condominiums or investing their wealth outside of their region. At the very least, if the public is to subsidise the private sector, then conditions need to be placed on where and how profits are spent so that the objective of regional development is attained. The national interest then could be quantified and evaluated.

The third fallacy of this doomsday rationale is that water entitlements are a tradeable commodity. Indeed, the argument that markets allocate resources most efficiently holds true even in the case of our most precious resource - water. An irrigator can sell some or all of their entitlements on the market if they so choose and buy them back at a later stage if it suits their business needs. When the Commonwealth buys entitlements, there is nothing to stop a willing seller to become a willing buyer, negating the impacts (if any) of the governments purchase. The only thing that is happening is that the total consumptive pool has reduced at catchment scale, and those distributional impacts are dispersed, not isolated to any one community.

Finally, it is important to note that a water entitlement does not always yield the physical volume of water attached to an entitlement. How much water an entitlement physically obtains in a given year is dependent on how much water is in the system, seasonal conditions, and other conditions placed on the entitlement. Hence, the 2750GL of entitlements held by the Commonwealth does not mean the river system gets an additional 2750GL of water in it each and every year.

The Commonwealth's environmental water holdings have to abide by the same conditions as irrigators do as these rules are attached to the entitlement. Some of the entitlements purchased are low security and have been defined as sub-prime water assets. The Commonwealth is in essence, an irrigator, but of wetlands and rivers. A less than optimal outcome given that river regulation is the leading cause of environmental decline. Instead of trying to return rivers to some level of naturalness, the opposite has happened. The environment has to abide by the principles of irrigated agriculture.

Conclusions: Lessons for the future

The primary emphasis of this case study is that what has been touted as a water 'reform' is in large part a centralised continuation of programs that already existed under a cooperative model of federation. But without State buy-in. The problem of governing water is not solved by large sums of centralised money. It is a governance problem of contested ideas, values and objectives. Effective multi-jurisdictional governance of Australia's natural resources requires that all governments have a stake in contributing to 'serving the national interest'.

Each jurisdiction has to relinquish some of its parochial jurisdictional interests so that the whole is greater than the sum of the parts. The federal system in Australia is one where cooperative models, as cumbersome as they are, deliver the best national outcomes. Centralisation of power has:

- marginalised and disempowered local voices;
- amplified the voices of powerful vested interests and elites with an interest in profit maximisation, diminishing other values;
- encouraged gaming and cost shifting by State governments; and
- undermined strategic thinking in favour of politicisation based on ideological differences rather than a focus on good governance and policy processes to resolve complex environmental problems (Samnakay, 2021).

Policy principles and designs need to be contested and debated. Policy experimentation and innovation needs to be encouraged guided by nationally agreed overarching frameworks. Adaptation and agility need to be part of the policy-making process rather than locking in large expensive projects which are fixed over time. The current mantra is to "stay the course". In an environment where climate change is already disrupting our understanding of natural systems, 'change is coming – get used to it' should be the mantra. The idea that water governance can be "addressed once and for all" is a gross injustice to the nation and a falsity. The oft used term 'water security' locks in a sense of entitlement rather than seeing water as central to multiple values including of justice, equity, human rights, cultural heritage, sustainability and of regional economies – that all need to be considered.

The Commonwealth can play a very constructive role as an agent of change. Facilitating frameworks and funding joint initiatives. It can not be an authority figure where it has none. There are many examples where the Commonwealth can provide large investments in funds with well-negotiated but detailed objectives. When tied to performance measures supported by regular policy evaluations, it is possible to achieve something greater than the sum of the parts. These cooperative mechanisms have been used before in competition policy reforms, in forestry reforms and in the NWI.

The mechanisms for governing the waters of MDB were already in place. A modest investment by the Commonwealth could have fast-tracked programs. In retrospect, the Commonwealth's exorbitant expenditure of public funds through a federal take-over has created a burgeoning bureaucracy and significant allocation of funds to private interests. The environment meanwhile continues to lose.

References

Besser, L. (2017, July 24.). Pumped. In S. Ferguson (Producer) Four Corners provided a detailed account of impropriety in spending of Commonwealth water reform funds. Four Corners. ABC Television. https://www.abc.net.au/4corners/pumped/8727826

Beasley, R. (2021). *Dead in the Water: A Very Angry Book about Our Greatest Environmental Catastrophe... the Death of the Murray-Darling Basin* (Vol. 296). Allen & Unwin. https://www.allenandunwin.com/browse/books/academic-professional/politics-government/Dead-in-the-Water-Richard-Beasley-9781760878450

Bettles, C. (2016, December 14). Are frogs killing regional growth. *Farmonline National.* https://www.farmonline.com.au/story/4356187/are-frogs-killing-regional-growth/

Botterill, L. C. (2016). Agricultural policy in Australia: deregulation, bipartisanship and agrarian sentiment. *Australian Journal of Political Science, 51*(4), 667-682. https://doi.org/10.1080/10361146.2016.1239567

COAG. (2004, June 25). *Intergovernmental Agreement on a National Water Initiative*. Council of Australian Governments, P.M. & C. https://www. pc.gov.au/inquiries/completed/water-reform/national-water-initiative-agreement-2004.pdf

CSIRO (2012). *Assessment of the ecological and economic benefits of environmental water in the Murray–Darling Basin*. CSIRO Water for a Healthy Country National Research Flagship, Australia. https://www.mdba.gov.au/sites/default/ files/archived/basinplan/2017-Assessment_Ecological_Economic_Benefits.pdf

Howard, J. (Hon). (2007, January 25). *A National Plan for Water Security. Address to the National Press Club*. Australian Parliament House.

https://parlinfo.aph.gov.au/parlInfo/download/media/pressrel/K81M6/upload_ binary/k81m68.pdf;fileType=application%2Fpdf#search=%22media/ pressrel/K81M6%22

Loch, A., Wheeler, S., Boxall, P., Hatton-Macdonald, D., & Bjornlund, H. (2014). Irrigator preferences for water recovery budget expenditure in the Murray-Darling Basin, Australia. *Land Use Policy*, *36*, 396-404. https:// doi.org/10.1016/j.landusepol.2013.09.007

M. D. B. A. (2010). Guide to the proposed Basin Plan. *Murray–Darling Basin Authority, Canberra*. https://www.mdba.gov.au/publications/archived-information/basin-plan-archives/guide-proposed-basin-plan

M. D. B. A. (2011). The Living Murray Story—One of Australia's Largest River Restoration Projects. *(Murray–Darling Basin Authority, publication no: 157/11)*. https://www.mdba.gov.au/sites/default/files/pubs/The-Living-Murray-story.pdf

MDBMC (Murray-Darling Basin Ministerial Council). (1996). *Setting the cap: report of the Independent Audit Group*. https://www.mdba.gov.au/sites/ default/files/archived/cap/SETTING_THE_CAP.pdf

Painter, M. (1996, January 1). The Council of Australian Governments and intergovernmental relations: a case of cooperative federalism. *Publius: The Journal of Federalism*, *26*(2), 101-120. https://doi.org/10.1093/ oxfordjournals.pubjof.a029844

Quiggin, J. (2012). Why the Guide to the Proposed Basin Plan failed, and what can be done to fix it. In T. Mallawaarachchi & S. Chambers (Eds.), *Water Policy Reform: Lessons in Sustainability from the Murray–Darling Basin (pp. 49-60)*. Edward Elgar. https://doi.org/10.4337/9781781000328.00014

Samnakay, N. (2021). A framework for analysing and informing Australia's National strategic natural resource management policies. *Australasian Journal of Environmental Management, 28*(3), 267-286. https://doi.org/10.1080/14486563.2021.1959427

South Australia (2019, January 29). *Murray-Darling Basin Royal Commission Report*. Brett Walker SC (Commissioner). https://cdn.environment.sa.gov.au/environment/docs/murray-darling-basin-royal-commission-report.pdf

The Age. (2007, April 16). *Water reform should not get bogged down by politics*, Editorial opinion.

https://www.theage.com.au/opinion/water-reform-should-not-get-bogged-down-by-politics-20070416-ge4o4w.html .

Wentworth Group of Concerned Scientists. (2020, August). *Assessment of river flows in the Murray-Darling Basin: Observed versus expected flows under the Basin Plan 2012-2019*, Sydney. https://wentworthgroup.org/wp-content/uploads/2020/08/MDB-flows.pdf

Wheeler, S. A., Carmody, E., Grafton, R. Q., Kingsford, R. T., & Zuo, A. (2020). The rebound effect on water extraction from subsidising irrigation infrastructure in Australia. *Resources, Conservation and Recycling, 159*, 104755. https://doi.org/10.1016/j.resconrec.2020.104755

Williams, J., & Grafton, R. Q. (2019). Missing in action: Possible effects of water recovery on stream and river flows in the Murray–Darling Basin, Australia. *Australasian Journal of Water Resources, 23*(2), 78-87. https://doi.org/10.1080/13241583.2019.1579965

Wittwer, G., & Dixon, J. (2013). Effective use of public funding in the Murray-Darling Basin: A comparison of buybacks and infrastructure upgrades. *Australian Journal of Agricultural and Resource Economics, 57*(3), 399-421. https://doi.org/10.1111/1467-8489.12001

CASE STUDY 3

Out of the ashes of and biochar of Narrogin – a new attempt at biofuels in WA

Simon Dawkins

Preface

There has been a strong interest in landcare in the WA Wheatbelt for decades following the large-scale clearing encouraged by the State Government. The subsequent emergence of low-lying areas becoming saline due to absence of trees became a key issue of land management with reports declaring that millions of hectares would become badly impacted. Added to this was the damaging wind erosion which removed topsoil on productive farms.

The growing awareness of these problems resulted in a strong desire to identify solutions to correct this imbalance. After a range of solutions were trialled, the planting of trees became seen as an important source of remediation and protection by lowering the water table and reducing wind speed. The problem however was – how to engage farmers in the widespread planting of trees on productive land.

The answer was to be found in the incentivisation of tree planting programs that sought to achieve a similar financial return as grain and livestock programs. After this context was established, it was followed by the identification of processes that might convert harvested biomass into valuable products such as biofuels, electricity, and biochar. A trial processing plant was established in 2006 at Narrogin and it ran long enough to provide proof of concept but was closed. The reasons for the ultimate failure of the trial processing plant are discussed along with suggestions for development of a bioenergy industry into the future.

Introduction

Andrea Gaynor summed up the situation in the Griffith Review "Faced with growing economic pressures as well as problems of salinity, erosion and other forms of land degradation, Wheatbelt farmers increasingly looked for ways to maintain efficient production while conserving the soil. Some turned to oil mallees for biofuel to diversify farm income and reduce wind erosion and salinity; by 2013, over 30 million trees had been planted across the state, many in the Wheatbelt. Construction of an integrated mallee processing plant that would produce eucalyptus oil, activated charcoal and heat for electricity generation was completed at Narrogin in 2006, but closed in 2011. With little political will to develop the industry, farmers were left with trees but no market for them." (Gaynor, 2015).

This passage from Andrea Gaynor's contribution to "Looking West", a special edition of the Griffith Review, follows her description of the way in which the rate of clearing land for cropping was accelerated during the 1950's and then into the long period of Liberal State government under Premier Sir David Brand (1959-1971). During that time Brand promoted the idea of extensive clearing and set a target of 1 Million acres per year. This greatly increased the area under crops but also created the problems noted by Gaynor.

Gaynor also highlights that the rate of clearing was also

enhanced by the tendency to engage large enterprises from the USA to undertake the task, particularly around Esperance, similar to the way in which successive State Governments pursued the opening up of the mining sector, by creating special acts of parliament to secure the interest of international companies in the Sate's mineral wealth.

While farmers became the target of criticism for conducting bad practices on the land, it was the extremely ruthless way in which the clearing was required to be executed that should be acknowledged. Often the complete clearing of the landscape was required leaving very little in the way of remnant bush. The negative long-term impact of this total clearing approach across the wheatbelt was generally acknowledged a decade after the clearing had taken place. Various schemes were developed to reduce the impact of salinity including drains that criss-crossed the properties effectively reducing the available land for cropping and impacting on the efficient harvesting by large equipment.

The Oil Mallee Association

It was a farmer with forestry training, Don Stanley, who initiated a discussion with the then head of the Department of Conservation and Land Management, Dr Syd Shea, and developed a landscape scale plan to put trees back into the landscape. This idea of using the trees for environmental benefit was coupled with a determination to make the trees pay their way, in other words meet the opportunity cost of displacing cropping with trees. As it was not possible at the time to allocate a financial benefit from carbon sequestration or the environmental benefits of the trees, it was necessary to develop a way of using the biomass for commercial purposes. The initial product to be envisaged was eucalyptus oil but from very early there was a desire to utilise the biomass for regional bioenergy production.

An association of interested farmers, led by Don Stanley, created the Oil Mallee Association of WA (OMA) to represent those that were interested in the idea of agroforestry and taking up the opportunity to receive low cost or even free seedlings, provided by the Commonwealth Government for planting across their properties. Within a few years the membership had risen to over 1000 farmers, approximately 25% of the total number of Wheatbelt farmers. Each farmer provided with seedlings entered into a contract with the OMA or its affiliated regional bodies to oblige them to re-engage if and when a system emerged to provide a carbon value the trees. In many cases a forestry harvest plan was created to guide the future transport vehicles that were anticipated to take the biomass to a processing facility. During these early stages, experienced forestry experts led and managed the OMA and this was evident from the nature of the contracts and the establishment of a sophisticated locational and contact database.

A significant period of advocacy and lobbying followed to bring about adoption of integrated tree planting in low rainfall areas of the WA Wheatbelt with an increasing amount of research indicating that bioenergy could provide a financial return to mallee growers.

As reflected in a study by the Joint Venture Agroforestry Program (JVAP), a program funded by three agricultural research organisations including RIRDC (Rural Industries Research and Development Corporation), the opportunity for the exploitation of short rotation woody crops for bioenergy was identified in 1996. Later studies (e.g. Powell & RIRDC, 2009), following the Australia's response to the 1998 UN Climate conference in Japan and the creation of the Kyoto Protocol, suggested that a significant amount of energy could be created from bioenergy to help meet the 2% Renewable energy target set by Australia.

The origins of the Narrogin ITP

In 2002 it was proposed by the OMA and others that an Integrated Tree Processing (ITP) plant was required to test the using of biomass sourced from the coppicing of plantations of mallee eucalypts planted on farms to produce bioenergy, activated carbon and eucalyptus oil. The creation of an ITP plant at Narrogin was an election promise of the incoming Gallop State Labor Government in 2001. By 2004 further studies noted that the market for bioenergy alone may not be sufficient, under the regulatory conditions of the day, to drive a new program of agroforestry for farmers and other benefits would be needed to drive commerciality of the program.

The features of the Narrogin project were described in a report by Florasearch for the South Australian centre for Natural Resource Management:

> "The development of an integrated wood processing or tree processing (IWP or ITP) demonstration plant at Narrogin in WA has been reported in depth by Western Power (2006) and Enecon (2001). Most of the engineering of the IWP plant was completed in 2005 and tested during 2006. The concept is based on utilising in-field chipping harvest technologies to deliver 20,000 tonnes of chipped mallee (Eucalyptus spp.) wood, twigs and leaves to the plant per annum for processing to produce 7.5 GWh/year of electricity, 690 tonnes/ year of activated carbon and 210 tonnes/year of eucalyptus oil. The IWP plant incorporates a fluidised bed carbonising plant, steam distillation plant, thermal gasifier spent leaf combustor plant and a 1 MW steam turbine power generation plant. Additional benefits will be derived from a greenhouse gas abatement scheme from renewable energy generation, rootmass fixation and standing woody crop biomass" (*Hobbs et al.*, 2014).

The 'additional benefits' mentioned in this report could however only be contemplated through a market for carbon abatement and that had yet to be established. The Carbon Rights Bill (WA) had been drafted in 2001 and the Act was passed in 2003 providing some expectation that carbon sequestration would be recognised in mallee plantings and therefore attract additional payments to farmers as a result. However, at this stage, it had not been envisaged how carbon in cyclically coppiced crops would be treated.

One interesting influence at this point also was the insistence by the Australian Greens in the Commonwealth Parliament that bioenergy could only be created from the by-product of other operations and that dedicated plantings were not acceptable. It had therefore been required that the multiple product approach be adopted, and in this case that the production of eucalyptus oil was required, with the by-product of chipped material being made into bioenergy.

Soon after commissioning of the plant, the balance of power in the Senate changed and the Federal Government was able to override this technical requirement in the legislation and enable the production of bioenergy from coppiced mallee plantings without the necessity to prove it was created from a waste product. Indeed, this attitude to bioenergy by some environmental groups is based on a very precautionary approach which does not recognise bioenergy as a carbon neutral product. Despite generally accepted decisions by the International Energy Agency and the UNFCCC itself, doubt remains in certain quarters over the legitimacy of the carbon neutrality of bioenergy. The principal basis on which carbon neutrality exists is the assumption that whatever wood product is used in producing bioenergy, the emissions are subsequently absorbed by plants and the system replenishes itself, notwithstanding the lag implicit in this cycle.

Successful trials were undertaken at the plant after modifications to the innovative pyrolysis process and certain safety features added including additional in person monitoring. These changes created the need for additional personnel on site and increased the cost of operation significantly.

The closure of the Narrogin ITP

At this very late stage, Verve, the State Government energy agency responsible for accelerating renewable energy, attempted to find co-investors in the project with no success. The project was officially closed, and the site eventually sold some years later. The estimated cost of the project was $20M with the process managed entirely by Verve. A fairly blunt assessment of the project was made by the State Government Department of Agriculture and Food in a Biomass Scoping Study: Opportunities of agriculture in WA" Bulletin 4862 in 2014.

> "A 1MW integrated wood processing (IWP) demonstration plant was completed in Narrogin in 2006 but is not functional in 2014. Western Power lost the drive to continue the process after contributing half the $20 million spent on the Narrogin plant mainly due to technical difficulties. Analysis of the reasons for not proceeding suggests the decision to attempt to build a plant integrating three separate technologies was overly ambitious. Had the proponents commissioned each technology separately with the ultimate aim of integrating the three once each part was proven, this plant may have been viable." (Brooksbank *et al.*, 2014)

The creation of a transformational technology that stimulated agroforestry for environmental benefit and profitability was abandoned even after a successful period of operation. There were probably other reasons for the failure, including an unrealistic setting of safety standards that limited the operation, created a high level of staffing and the incorporation of new untested technologies such as the CSIRO fluidised bed which, it is believed, proved to be unsuccessful.

The closure of the Narrogin ITP coincided with a termination of the Commonwealth and State programs that had provided low-cost seedlings. While 21 Million mallee seedlings had been distributed, the confidence in the future viability of the bioenergy program was diminished by the early closure of the Narrogin ITP.

There had also been an expectation that carbon sequestration programs based on permanent plantings of trees would be available. Indeed, a Japanese company, the Kansai Electric Company of Japan, undertook the planting of 1000 hectares of mallees in the northern wheatbelt and paid farmers for the use of their land. While this scheme was solely aimed at carbon sequestration rather than bioenergy, it provided leadership in the general enthusiasm for trees on farms.

At the same time, Ian Stanley, son of the late Don Stanley, helped create a pyrolysis processing system and acquired the patent for the process after he and others had optimised the way it operated. This also gave hope that something would happen in relation to mallees and bioenergy.

Implications for the regional bioenergy industry

The failure of the Narrogin ITP, while a relatively small project, had a significant negative impact on the momentum to create a bioenergy industry in Western Australia. The Cooperative Research Centre for Future Farm Industries (CRCFFI), which was established around this time to, in part, investigate the use of agroforestry for energy, failed to lift the level of interest of farmers to a significant extent. To the extent that the Narrogin ITP initially provided a beacon of hope and influenced a significant proportion of Wheatbelt farmers, it is a White Elephant worth noting.

One origin of its ultimate failure might be attributed to the effective advocacy by a farmer group (the OMA) which, while pushing hard for its establishment, was unclear about the likelihood of success. However, it secured sufficient political support from a then opposition political party to ensure it was created after they won office.

In addition, the level of control by a single government utility, one created to promote renewable energy, removed it from a necessary degree of consultation and continuous feedback from specialist and other experienced commercial managers. To some extent also, the potential benefits and impact were exaggerated by the community and industry advocates and the failure to meet expectations reduced the likelihood of another attempt at regional bioenergy, until the project was a distant memory.

Climate change policy

One interesting aspect of this experiment in regional bioenergy is the relationship between the capacity and willingness to initiate programs of this sort in an atmosphere of doubt and confusion related to climate change policy development. It is likely that consistent and well supported public attitudes are an essential component of efforts to achieve success in public investment in climate change projects.

As can be seen from the chart below, the national appetite for climate change policies was very volatile during the period in question and became distinctly unsure when the responsibility for a consistent national policy was effectively transferred to the Commonwealth by the States via COAG (Council of Australian Governments). Despite the rhetoric, or perhaps because of it, the public became increasingly uncertain of climate change policies and this uncertainty was exploited politically to undermine development of a national approach. Without a fully functioning carbon policy and market for carbon credits, developments such as Narrogin did not provide a level of confidence that income would flow from the sale of carbon offsets to companies seeking compliance with yet to be established restrictions on emissions based on legislated targets.

Geels Transition theory (addressed later) suggests that a compatible policy framework and supportive social attitudes social are crucial to the development of large-scale projects.

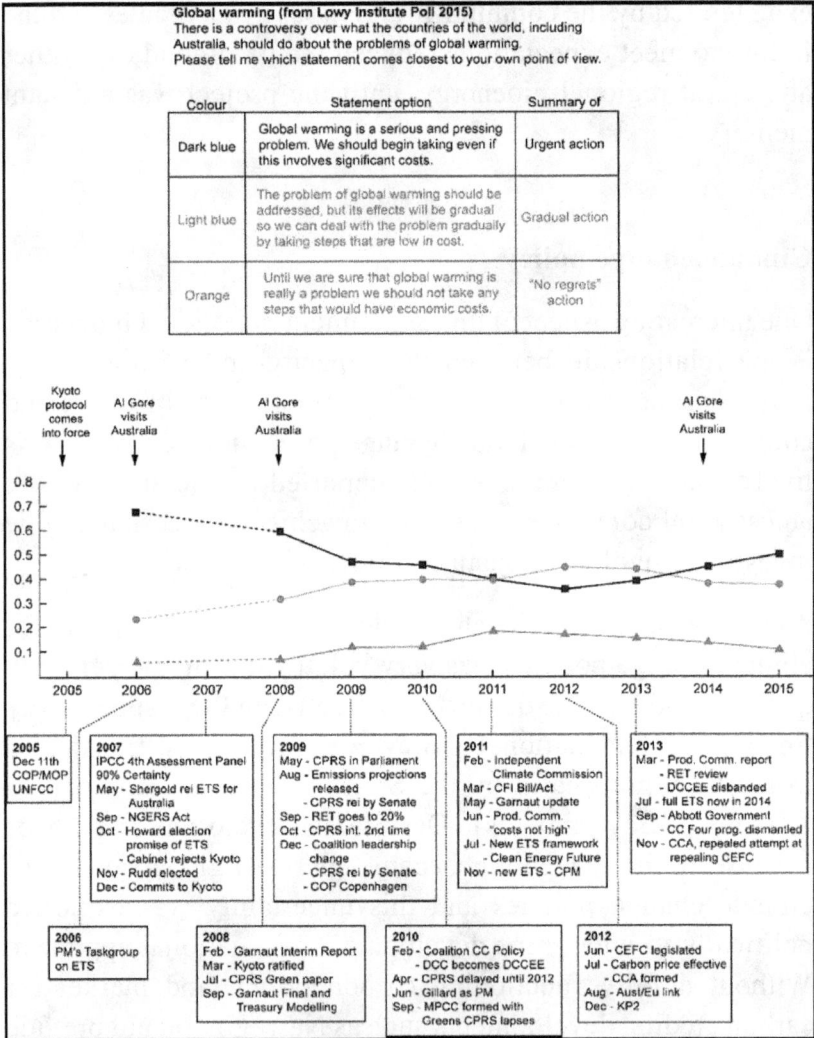

This chart is derived from Figure 3.2 in Dawkins 2020, PhD thesis The Sustainability of Carbon Mitigation in Dryland Farming Systems: The Oil Mallee Case Study.

Parallel developments

Despite the closure of the Narrogin plant, there continued to be interest in pursuing the idea biomass to energy. Several areas of research have looked at different aspects of the challenge to use woody biomass grown on farmland to produce energy and perhaps an important incidental by-product, biochar. A pyrolysis process, which entails heating biomass in the absence of oxygen, releases the volatiles embedded in the wood for purification and are captured as biofuel. What remains is biochar, a very stable form of carbon. There have been developments in biochar which can now be considered as representing negative carbon emissions when produced in the production of biofuels and displacing fossil fuels. Large international companies are purchasing these "drawdown" negative carbon credits and the demand should increase. The use of biochar in agriculture has also been attracting significant interest for many years, with many studies demonstrating the many beneficial uses of biochar in soil improvement.

The CRC Future Farm Industries (CRCFFI) produced significant case studies and reviews of technologies. One such study in 2013/14, funded by Airbus, produced a feasibility study of the production of sustainable aviation fuels from mallee biomass plus several very valuable economic studies on the positive impact of integrated agroforestry on the farming enterprise. (Goss, 2014).

More recently, several studies on the feasibility of a biofuels industry based on mallee biomass have been initiated. In addition, other bioenergy projects are being developed using municipal waste and other sources of vegetation. These studies are also seeking to test the financial feasibility of producing biofuels from existing mallee agroforestry and are building their case on the extensive research, and failures, conducted over 30 years. This will be discussed later.

The climate change policy context

A very different context to the period of the Narrogin trial on climate change action has emerged, even though government policy has not changed significantly over many years. In particular the resources sector is keen to seek offsets for their emissions from production. Programs for creating offset programs through permanent reforestation has become less viable and is under scrutiny but are supported by the demand for offset credits and a high 'voluntary' price. However, of particular concern is the switch in land use from agriculture to unproductive reafforestation when introducing large scale permanent 'block' planting can cover whole properties.

The response to the impact of this practice on land use was the introduction of planning regulations which limit the extent of carbon plantings on high grade agricultural land. Special Purpose Plan 2.5 recently introduced by the WA Planning Commission states that approval of tree planting on valuable agricultural land is required if it exceeds 10% of the property. These regulations are unlikely to impact on the integrated agroforestry model.

The production of biofuels which displace fossil fuels can possibly create an acceleration of carbon credits. The "King" review of the Emission Reduction Fund (ERF) recommended that fuel switching (from fossil fuel to renewable fuel) should be accredited with an awarding of carbon credits whereas only renewable energy credits are available. The Commonwealth has endorsed this and other recommendations of the King Review but the changes are yet to be adopted.

In addition, other projects which have sought to demonstrate the potential of using biomass for energy had been initiated. Renergi Ltd, a company created out of a long terms research effort to commercialise biomass to energy technology has been recently funded to be part of a renewable energy program located at Collie, a site for energy generation traditionally from locally sourced coal.

Another example is Rainbow BeeEater Ltd which was created after a visit by a mallee farmer (Ian Stanley), a scientist and an engineer and uses a uniquely simplified system of producing syngas and biochar with biomass feedstock. This system has subsequently been installed at two large greenhouses in South Australia. For one project waste timber is transported from Melbourne and traded for the biochar produced which is incorporated into garden mulch. In other words, the feedstock is acquired at no cost! In addition, the "drawdown" credits are sold to international companies.

More importantly, the process of pyrolysis produces power to heat the greenhouse, and the carbon dioxide is pumped into the greenhouse to stimulate additional growth. This project may be replicated in Queensland using rampant and difficult to manage prickly pear as its feedstock. These commercial projects have taken off at least in part from the learnings of the Narrogin ITP failure, because the targeted transformational outcome is more achievable, rather than having to prove the technology.

One analysis of this difficulty of scaling for a specific purpose has been considered by Frank Geels, whose "transition theory" has been applied to many industries to understand the dynamic of change from one level of adoption to another (Geels, 2018). In relation to mallee integrated agroforestry, the complex transitions required to bring the industry up to scale and widespread adoption have been analysed. The diagram below was included in a PhD thesis by the author in an attempt to understand the many influences that impede and encourage advancement of an idea from the 'micro' level to the 'meso' level and finally to "macro" and landscape adoption.

The influences on transition include socio economic impacts on development of the underlying carbon policy that can levelise the cost of different fuels under a climate change framework and drive or inhibit adoption. It identifies the necessity of experimentation and trialling of technologies and the subsequent adoption of supportive industry policies at crucial stages to ensure lasting adoption in a competitive and market-based environment.

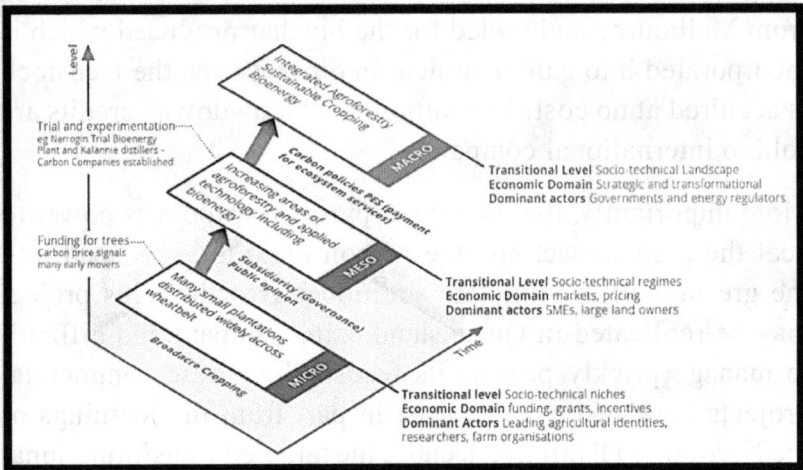

Trial and experimentation—
eg Narrogin Trial Bioenergy
Plant and Kalannie distillers –
Carbon Companies established

Integrated Agroforestry Sustainable Cropping Bioenergy

Carbon policies PES (payment for ecosystem services)

Increasing areas of agroforestry and applied technology including bioenergy

Subsidiarity (Governance) Public opinion

Funding for trees—
Carbon price signals
many early movers

Many small plantations distributed widely across wheatbelt

Broadacre Cropping

MACRO
MESO
MICRO

Level

Time

Transitional Level Socio-technical Landscape
Economic Domain Strategic and transformational
Dominant actors Governments and energy regulators

Transitional Level Socio-technical regimes
Economic Domain markets, pricing
Dominant actors SMEs, large land owners

Transitional level Socio-technical niches
Economic Domain funding, grants, incentives
Dominant Actors Leading agricultural identities,
researchers, farm organisations

Adapting Geels transition theory to mallee agroforestry, (Dawkins, 2020)

The prospects for a new Narrogin emerge in 2022

More than a decade after the Narrogin plant closed, there are moves to establish a Biorefinery in the shire. Future Energy Australia (FEA) is planning to use biomass from various sources to produce a renewable diesel as a carbon neutral alternative for high diesel consuming industries such as mining, construction, transport aviation and electricity generation. The information released at the launch on 1 June 2022 states that there will be over $100M investment with 130 direct and indirect jobs and utilisation of 10,000 hectares of oil mallees for coppicing. Wood vinegar (used in fertilisers and other agricultural uses) plus biochar will also be produced.

FEA is a joint venture between the Frontier Impact Group and Carnarvon Energy Ltd. (frontierimpact.com.au, carnarvon.com.au)

While this project on its own does not necessarily indicate that the transition to the 'macro' level might be achieved, it does reveal the possible impact of the change in 'socio technical regimes' and the importance of government and the existing and anticipated changes in policies that support sustainable bioenergy.

However, what might indicate transition to the Geels 'macro' level is the significant level of new interest in biofuels by a range of companies and financial institutions. Among those indicating interest in a wheatbelt biofuel industry based significantly on oil mallees is a consortium of the ANZ Bank, Inpex and Qantas with a very large-scale proposal for production of renewable biofuel. Other projects are also being developed but are at an earlier stage of development and have not been publicly announced.

Conclusion

In addition to the possibility of a growing interest by governments and proposed changes to regulation of carbon credit generation in biofuels and biochar, attention has been drawn to the heavy reliance of Australia on imported fuel. Indeed, 'fuel security' may well become one of those regulatory issues that helps shift the industry into a broad scale industry.

While the Narrogin ITP or IWPw as a failure and a White Elephant, for many reasons it also could have been more properly seen as a necessary step towards realisation of a new rural industry with multiple benefits. It was a creature and victim of politics, climate change policy inertia, bureaucratic inflexibility, and inexperience. Narrogin was a world class initiative which was planned to break new ground in terms of its application in a low rainfall agricultural region but was abandoned too quickly amid overly ambitious claims of its potential impact - while in fact it was an early trial and it needed to be seen as just that.

References

Brooksbank, K., Lever, M., Paterson, H., & Weybury, M. (2014, August). Biomass scoping study: Opportunities for agriculture in Western Australia. WA Dept. of Agriculture & Food. https://www.agric.wa.gov.au/sites/ gateway/files/Biomass%20scoping%20study%20-%20opportunities%20 for%20agriculture%20in%20Western%20Australia%20-%20Bulletin%20 4862%20%28PDF%202.2MB%29.pdf

Dawkins, S. (2020). The Sustainability of Carbon Mitigation in Dryland Farming Systems: The Oil Mallee Case Study (Doctoral dissertation, Curtin University). http://hdl.handle.net/20.500.11937/83307

Gaynor, A. (2015). How to eat a wilderness: the past and future of the Wheatbelt. *Griffith Review*, (47), 169-180. https://search.informit.org/ doi/10.3316/ielapa.020947590109948

Geels, F. W. (2018). Socio-technical transitions to sustainability. In *Oxford research encyclopedia of environmental science*. https://doi.org/10.1093/ acrefore/9780199389414.013.587

Goss, K. (2014). *Sustainable mallee jet fuel: sustainability and life cycle assessment for supply to Perth airport, Western Australia.* Future Farm Industries CRC.

Hobbs, T. J., Neumann C. R., Tucker M., Mazanec R., Bennell M., & McKenna D. (2014). *Performance of Native Plant Species in South Australian Woody Crop Trials – FloraSearch 4.* DEWNR Technical Report 2014/15. Government of South Australia, through Department of Environment, Water and Natural Resources, Adelaide & Future Farm Industries Cooperative Research Centre, Perth. https://data.environment.sa.gov.au/Content/

Publications/FloraSearch-4-DEWNR-TR-2014-15.pdf

Powell, J. & Rural Industries Research and Development Corporation (Australia) & Joint Venture Agroforestry Program (Australia). (2009). *Fifteen years of the Joint Venture Agroforestry Program: foundation research for Australia's tree crop revolution.* RIRDC

Photo: A group visit the Narrogin ITP in about 2006.

CASE STUDY 4

White Elephants in Local Government: Australian Municipal Mergers as State Government Failure

Brian Dollery

Introduction

In stark contrast to most other developed countries, Australian local government policy has been characterised by a heavy reliance on structural change based on compulsory council consolidation (see, for instance, Dollery, *et al.*, 2008, Dollery, *et al.*, 2012, Dollery, *et al.*, 2020, Dollery & Robbotti, 2008, and Faulk & Hicks, 2011). Indeed, Anne Vince (1997, p. 151) has described forced amalgamation as 'a golden thread which runs through Australian local government history'. With the sole exception of Western Australia (WA) (Dollery & Tiley, 2015), all Australian state and territory local government systems have undergone municipal merger programs. Moreover, even in WA, the state government has sought (but failed) to impose municipal mergers on unwilling Perth councils (Drew & Dollery, 2014a).

It is important to distinguish between municipal mergers and other forms of municipal reform. A useful way of considering structural reform through council amalgamation is to adopt the reform typology developed by Dollery *et al.* (2008) in their comparative study of Anglosphere municipal systems in Australia, Britain, Canada, Ireland, New Zealand and the United States. Dollery *et al.* (2008) distinguish between five discrete categories of municipal reform. Financial reform comprises modifying the financial circumstances of local government, usually focused on changes to revenue (i.e. "own-source" revenue and intergovernmental transfers), expenditure (i.e. financial responsibilities and financial restrictions) and financial management. Functional reform involves changes in the number or kinds of functions performed by local government, including realigning functions between local government and other levels of government. Jurisdictional reforms comprise changes to the authority and autonomy of local government, including general competency powers and specific bylaw-making powers. Organisational and managerial reforms involve changes to the administrative, executive and management processes of local councils. Finally, structural reform encompasses changes to the boundaries, numbers and types of local authority, including through compulsory council consolidation.

Notwithstanding the heavy reliance by policy makers on forced mergers in Australian local government, compulsory amalgamation remains controversial (see, for instance, Dollery *et al.*, 2012). Advocates of amalgamation have typically argued that it represents an effective method of improving the operational efficiency of local councils, enhancing their administrative and technical capacity, generating cost savings, strengthening strategic decision-making and fostering greater political power. By contrast, opponents of consolidation typically underline the divisive nature of amalgamations, the absence of supportive empirical evidence, the equivocal outcomes observed in case studies and the diminution of local democracy. Moreover, the case for structural change through municipal mergers is often met with the claim that intermunicipal cooperation through resource-sharing, shared services and other forms of council collaboration represents a superior means of securing any benefits attendant upon council size and its scale of operations (Dollery *et al.*, 2006).

This chapter considers municipal amalgamation as an exemplar of the 'white elephant' policy phenomenon in Australian local government reform programs. In Australia, municipal mergers have typically met the definition of white elephants insofar as they are consistently poorly executed, their costs almost invariably exceed their purported benefits, the purported benefits are typically exaggerated and often their real intent is political rather than the broader public interest.

The chapter consists of three main parts. Section 2 offers a synoptic account of the chief characteristics of Australian municipal merger programs, as well as a summary of trends in the number of Australian local authorities from 1910 to 2020. Section 3 considers two of the largest and most controversial municipal merger programs in recent history - the 2008 Queensland forced amalgamation program and the 2016 New South Wales (NSW) compulsory council consolidation episode – as illustrative examples of Australian municipal merger programs and then examines empirical evidence on their outcomes. The chapter ends in section 4 with some brief concluding remarks on the policy lessons that can be drawn from white elephant amalgamation programs.

Characteristics of Australian Compulsory Council Consolidation Programs

Australian compulsory council consolidation programs follow a common pattern (Dollery *et al.,* 2012). In the first instance, newly-elected state governments typically complain publically of local government inefficiency and a concomitant lack of municipal financial viability. An 'independent' inquiry is then customarily established to consider methods of improving local government. After a period of deliberation, the inquiry commonly releases a discussion paper (or papers), followed by an interim report and then a final report. These reports consistently recommend forced amalgamation. After a token period of 'public consultation', the proposed mergers proceed, notwithstanding widespread public opposition.

After a compulsory council consolidation program has been instituted, a common pattern is also evident (Dollery *et al.,* 2012). Ongoing public discontent with council mergers typically endures, often for many years. This sometimes results in de-amalgamation, as in Queensland (see, for example, De Souza *et al.,* 2015). In addition, there is never any public assessment of the costs of mergers to affected councils or to their local communities, despite the fact that little or no improvement in the operational efficiency or financial viability of amalgamated councils is observed. After a period of years, the same cycle reoccurs.

If we consider Australian state and territory local government reform programs over the past several decades, we can discern five common features (Bell *et al.,* 2016; Dollery, *et al.,* 2008; Dollery *et al.,* 2020; Dollery, *et al.,* 2011). Firstly, although state and territory governments typically rule out forced amalgamation at the outset, many municipal reform programs metamorphose into compulsory consolidation programs, as evidenced in both the 2008 Queensland amalgamation program and the 2016 NSW municipal merger program. Secondly, Australian municipal reform processes focused on structural change rely heavily on forced mergers rather than other types of structural transformation, such as shared services. Thirdly, legislative coercion is commonly deployed by state governments to force amalgamation upon reluctant local councils designated for compulsory consolidation. Fourthly, various post-amalgamation measures are often employed to limit the negative short-run impact of mergers, especially constraints on increasing municipal rates, fees and charges. Finally, state governments never conduct formal evaluations of the outcomes of their compulsory council consolidation programs (Bell *et al.*, 2016).

Table 1 illustrates long-run trends in the number of Australian local authorities:

Table 1: Number of local councils in Australia, 1910–2020

	1910	1967	1982	1990	1995	2008	2012	2020
NSW	324	224	175	176	177	152	152	128
VIC	206	210	211	210	184	79	79	79
QLD	164	131	134	134	125	73	73	78
SA	175	142	127	n/a	119	68	68	68
WA	147	144	138	138	144	142	139	141
TAS	51	49	49	46	29	29	29	29
NT	0	1	6	22	63	16	16	17
TOTAL	**1,067**	**901**	**840**	**726**	**841**	**559**	**556**	**545**

Sources: Dollery, *et al.*, (2012); Australian Local Government Association (2020).

Several features can be identified in Table 1. Firstly, the total number of local authorities in Australia has decreased from 1,067 to 545 (a fall of 49 per cent) between 1910 and 2020 despite substantial population growth over the period. Some notable transient exceptions to this general trend occurred in the Northern Territory (NT), where the number of councils substantially increased from 22 in 1990 to 63 in 1995, but thereafter fell drastically. Major mergers occurred in NSW between 1967 and 1982 (a reduction from 224 to 175 councils) and again in 2016 (a further fall of 24 councils). A radical municipal merger program took place in Tasmania over the period 1990 to 1995 reducing the number of municipalities from 46 to 29 councils. Similarly, a period of major structural reform unfolded in Victoria from 1995 to 2007 (from 184 to 79 councils). Queensland experienced radical compulsory council consolidation in 2007, with a decrease from 125 to 73 councils. Finally, the NT underwent drastic amalgamation in 2008 (from 63 to 16 councils).

Forced Amalgamation Programs in New South Wales and Queensland

In order to understand the nature of Australian compulsory council consolidation programs and their outcomes, it is useful to consider two controversial recent large scale structural reform programs as illustrative examples: the 2008 Queensland council amalgamation process and the 2016 NSW municipal merger program.

2008 Queensland Amalgamation Program

In 2005, the initial significant step towards the 2008 Queensland municipal merger program was taken when the *Size, Shape and Sustainability* initiative (SSS) was introduced by the Queensland state government with the stated aim of fostering the formation of collaborative relationships between local authorities in the Queensland local government system. The SSS process sought to stimulate local councils to consider alternative options for structural reform (LGAQ, 2005). A 'guidelines kit' defined the objectives of the SSS process and proposed a number of financial sustainability indicators to be used to assess proposals (Dollery & Akimov, 2008). However, even though the SSS program was originally funded for five years, it was abruptly halted in April 2007 when the Queensland state government decided instead to pursue a forced amalgamation process (Dollery *et al.*, 2011).

In the immediate aftermath of the cancellation of the SSS process, the Queensland Local Government Reform Commission (QLGRC) was established to review 156

Queensland councils (Dollery, Ho Chong Mun & Alin, 2008). Brisbane City Council was excluded at the outset on grounds it had unique characteristics as the state capital of Queensland. In July 2007, the QLGRC (2007) issued a report recommending *inter alia* that Queensland councils be amalgamated into 73 new entities. These changes were claimed to optimise service delivery and improve collaboration with other levels of government to ensure 'sustainable and viable communities'.

In essence, the amalgamation program sought to simultaneously achieve both greater operational efficiency and enhanced financial sustainability (QLGRC 2007, p. 37). However, the QLGRC (2007) did not present any empirical evidence in support of its recommendations. Rather it claimed that its recommendations were justified because - according to a 2005 survey – five earlier municipal mergers in Queensland in the 1990s purportedly improved effectiveness. While shared service arrangements and multi-purpose joint local government boards were considered, these were eventually rejected (QLGRC, 2007).

The recommended municipal mergers occurred in March 2008, despite widespread opposition in the affected local council areas. Public dissatisfaction was exacerbated by the fact that the prescribed timeframe severely limited the opportunity for public involvement. In line with other commentators, Drew and Dollery (2014) argued that the Queensland state government acted in excessive haste to preclude opponents of forced amalgamation from organising effectively. In its defence, the QLGRC (2007) sought to rationslize the rapid pace of the merger process by claiming its benefits would be realised sooner!

Empirical Evaluation of the 2008 Queensland Municipal Merger Outcomes

To date, three empirical evaluations of the outcomes of the 2008 Queensland local government amalgamation program have been conducted. In the first place, Drew *et al.*, (2016a) examined whether the Queensland municipal mergers had lowered the operational costs of merged councils, given that the Queensland amalgamation program was based *inter alia* on the assumption that increased economies of scale attendant upon larger councils by population would generate cost savings.

In their study, Drew *et al.* (2016a) examined pre-amalgamation (2006/07) data and post-amalgamation (2009/10) data for scale economies. For the 2006/07 data, evidence of scale economies was found for councils with populations up to 98,000 and thereafter diseconomies of scale for councils with larger aggregate populations. Eight percent of councils in 2006/07 (ten councils) – representing some 64% of the Queensland population – exhibited diseconomies of scale. For the 2009/10 data, the average cost curve remained almost stationary at 99,000 residents per council, but almost 25% of all councils (thirteen councils) were now found to exhibit diseconomies of scale. The compulsory municipal merger program had thus increased the proportion of Queensland residents in councils operating with diseconomies of scale to 84% and thereby failed in its intended aim of improving the efficiency of Queensland councils.

Secondly, McQuestin *et al.* (2017) investigated the claim by the Queensland state government that its compulsory council consolidation program would enhance the technical efficiency of the merged entities using intertemporal Data Envelopment Analysis over the period 2003 to 2013 inclusive. Their empirical evidence suggested that (a) in the financial year preceding the mergers, there was no statistically significant difference in the typical efficiency scores of amalgamated and non-amalgamated councils and (b) two years after the forced mergers the typical technical efficiency score of the amalgamated councils was well below that of the non-amalgamated cohort. McQuestin *et al.* (2017) argued this result could be attributed to increased staffing expenditure, although comparatively larger operational expenditure also served to diminish efficiency. McQuestin *et al.* (2017, p. 542) noted that Australian municipal merger programs, including the Queensland amalgamation, are based on projected savings 'strongly predicated on reduced staff expenditure once any moratorium on redundancy has expired'. This presumption was not borne out in Queensland.

Finally, Fellows, *et al.* (2021) investigated the impact of the 2008 Queensland municipal merger program on municipal efficiency by applying a geometric distance function-based efficiency analysis approach to panel data covering the period from 2006 to 2014. They found that the 2008 Queensland compulsory council consolidation program did not improve the technical efficiency of forcibly merged local councils. Given that the architects of the forced amalgamation program had claimed that compulsory council consolidation would enhance municipal efficiency, Fellows *et al.* (2021) contend that the program must thus be 'considered unsuccessful'. However, they note that their results did not indicate an overall fall in municipal efficiency, despite some councils experiencing substantial changes in their operational efficiency.

Fellows *et al.* (2021) argued further that the policy process underlying the Queensland forced amalgamation program may have been rushed for political reasons. They contend that this could have contributed to its failure by leaving inadequate time to refine individual merger proposals, thereby spawning an ill-designed council consolidation policy. They conclude that while compulsory municipal merger programs are clearly neither a 'magic bullet' solution to technical inefficiency in local government nor invariably worsen the problem in all cases, the empirical evidence demonstrates that they were an unfortunate policy instrument for Queensland local government.

2016 New South Wales Amalgamation Program

Over 17/18 August 2011, the (then) NSW Minister for Local Government Don Page convened a *Destination 2036* Workshop in Dubbo of all mayors and general managers from all NSW local councils. The major outcome of the *Destination 2036* Workshop lay in the establishment of an Independent Local Government Review Panel (ILGRP) to 'investigate and identify options for governance models, structural arrangements and voluntary boundary changes for local government in NSW' (NSW Division of Local Government, 2012).

In April 2013, the Panel published *Future Directions for NSW Local Government: Twenty Essential Steps* that outlined the 'latest thinking of the Independent Local Government Review Panel as it enters the final 3-4 months of its work program'. In the present context, the most salient feature of *Future Directions for NSW Local Government* was its focus on structural change through compulsory council consolidation, concentrated on local councils in metropolitan NSW, especially in the Greater Sydney region. The Panel (ILGRP, 2013, p. 9) noted that 'creating a sustainable system that can make the best use of limited resources and cope with the challenges of a changing world must involve some amalgamations of existing councils, large and small, urban and rural', emphasising that 'there is simply not enough revenue or sufficient numbers of skilled staff to sustain 152 councils across NSW'. Notwithstanding the radical nature of its forced amalgamation program, a striking characteristic of *Future Directions for NSW Local Government* is the lack of empirical evidence in support of compulsory mergers and concomitant claims that amalgamation would improve financial sustainability in NSW local government.

The Panel requested that the NSW Treasury Corporation (TCorp) prepare Financial Sustainability Reports for each of the 152 NSW councils. Given the centrality of financial sustainability, completed reports were required within a twelve-month period. This challenging timeframe resulted in TCorp relying heavily on the contentious work of the Queensland Treasury Corporation (QTC) that had produced regular financial sustainability reports on Queensland local authorities since July 2007 (TCorp, 2013, p. 20).

This was acknowledged by TCorp (2013, p. 21), which noted that its TCorp Financial Sustainability Reports had 'considered the work previously undertaken by other jurisdictions around Australia'. However, the TCorp reports ignored both the scholarly literature and international practice in other national jurisdictions. Ten financial sustainability ratios were calculated for the targeted councils by TCorp. After examining the Financial Sustainability Reports prepared by TCorp, the ILGRP concluded that they contained 'a disturbing picture of a local government system facing major financial problems with apparently little awareness of just how serious the situation has become' (ILGRP, 2013, p. 4). However, no attempt was made to analyse the appropriateness of either the ratios or the benchmarks employed.

Empirical Evaluation of the 2016 New South Wales Municipal Merger Outcomes

As we have seen from the 2008 Queensland experience, Australian local government structural reform programs are often based on the purported benefits of increased scale.

Drew *et al*., (2016b) investigated this question in the context of the NSW merger using Data Envelopment Analysis. They found empirical evidence that a significant proportion of municipalities scheduled for forced amalgamation already exceeded optimal scale and that the great majority of subsequently merged entities would thus suffer further decreasing returns to scale. These findings contrasted sharply with the claim made by the ILGRP that municipal mergers represented the optimal approach to capturing economies of scale in NSW local government.

Secondly, in their empirical analysis of economies of scale in NSW local government, Fahey *et al*. (2016) noted that since municipalities conduct multiple production activities, the relationship between expenditure and size is likely to vary based on each functional activity. Put differently, economies of scale, if they exist, may be 'service-specific' in that councils do not necessarily exhibit scale in all of their activities. Fahey *et al*. (2016) stratified their empirical results by council type (general-purpose councils and non-general-purpose councils) for each of the eleven municipal functional categories in NSW local government. For non-general purpose councils, potential economies of scale only occurred in the production of public order services and governance services, which represented only 6.7% of the municipal expenditure of these councils. For general purpose councils, they found that only public order, transport and economic affairs indicated potential for economies of scale. Fahey *et al*. (2016) thus concluded that their findings cast doubt on the potential for net cost savings from the NSW municipal merger program. Indeed, they found that for non-general-purpose councils, mergers would result in net diseconomies of scale. They drew the primary policy implication that inefficiency is minimised where councils are constituted at the smallest optimal size of any function exhibiting a decreasing average cost curve.

Finally, Drew and Dollery (2021) examined the outcome of the forced amalgamation of the Cootamundra and Gundagai shire councils into the Cootamundra Gundagai Regional Council (CGRC) in 2016. Prior to the compulsory consolidation of the CGRC, various documents and commissioned reports prepared by NSW government agencies, commercial consultants KPMG and the NSW Boundaries Commission Delegate all claimed that significant cost savings and other financial benefits would flow from the consolidated CGRC. Using data from the three post-merger financial years, Drew and Dollery (2021) examined these claims against observed financial and operational efficiency outcomes at the CGRC. Three different analyses were conducted: aggregate accounting measures were examined, financial ratio analysis was used for performance comparison, and operational efficiency was estimated using Data Envelopment Analysis. All three analyses decisively demonstrated that the CGRC had not only failed to reap the claimed cost savings and other financial benefits, but its fiscal performance had deteriorated sharply, even compared with other forcibly amalgamated NSW councils. In sum, the CGRC represents a clear case of a NSW state government white elephant.

Conclusions: Lessons for the Future

As we have seen, neither the international scholarly literature nor its Australian counterpart offers empirical support for the claimed efficacy of forced amalgamation as a means of improving municipal efficiency and enhancing municipal financial viability. The obvious implication of this weight of empirical evidence is that policy makers should avoid structural reform based on forced amalgamation and instead use other policy instruments. However, the history of compulsory council consolidation in Australia has vividly demonstrated that the absence of empirical evidence in favour of forced amalgamation has not deterred state or territory policy makers from their heavy reliance on amalgamation as a primary engine of local government reform.

Given the fact that in all state and territory jurisdictions local government is largely a 'creature of statute', and thus subject to the whim and fancy of state government regulators, it is difficult to conceive of an enduring method of preventing future episodes of forced amalgamation, short of constitutional change entrenching the independence of local government from state government. Moreover, little can be done to ameliorate the damage done by previous compulsory council consolidation programs. While de-amalgamation has been attempted following failed forced mergers, especially in the wake of the 2008 Queensland amalgamation program, the costs of council restoration have been prohibitive (Drew & Dollery, 2014b; 2015; De Souza *et al.*, 2015). Furthermore, in Queensland these costs have largely fallen on the demerged councils themselves in a brutal display of injustice.

References

Bell, B., Dollery, B., & Drew, J. (2016). Learning from Experience in NSW?. *Economic Papers: A journal of applied economics and policy, 35*(2), 99-111. https://doi.org/10.1111/1759-3441.12136

Faulk, D. G., & Hicks, M. J. (2011). *Local government consolidation in the United States*. Cambria Press.de Souza, S. V., Dollery, B. E., & Kortt, M. A. (2015). De-amalgamation in action: the Queensland experience. *Public Management Review, 17*(10), 1403-1424. https://doi.org/10.1080/1471903 7.2014.930506

Dollery, B., & Akimov, A. (2008). A Critical comment on the analysis of shared services in the Queensland Local Government Association's size, shape and sustainability program. *Accounting, Accountability & Performance, 14*(2), 29-44. *https://search.informit.org/doi/10.3316/informit.785056698579110*

Dollery, B., Byrnes, J., & Crase, L. (2008). Australian local government amalgamation: a conceptual analysis of population size and scale economies in municipal service provision. *Australasian Journal of Regional Studies, The, 14*(2), 167-175. https://www.anzrsai.org/assets/Uploads/PublicationChapter/262-Dolleryetal2.pdf

Dollery, B., Crase, L., & Johnson, A. (2006). *Australian local government economics*. UNSW Press.

Dollery, B., Garcea, J., & LeSage, E. C. (Eds.). (2008). *Local government reform: a comparative analysis of advanced Anglo-American countries*. Edward Elgar Publishing.

Dollery, B. E., Grant, B., & Kortt, M. A. (2012). *Councils in cooperation: Shared services and Australian local government*. Federation Press.

Dollery, B., Grant, B., & Kortt, M. (2013). An evaluation of amalgamation and financial viability in Australian local government. *Public Finance & Management, 13*(3), 215-238. https://www.researchgate.net/profile/Michael-Kortt/publication/255722306_An_Evaluation_of_Amalgamation_and_Financial_Viability_in_Australia_Local_Government/links/0046352323b21de0ce000000/An-Evaluation-of-Amalgamation-and-Financial-Viability-in-Australia-Local-Government.pdf?_sg%5B0%5D=started_experiment_milestone&origin=journalDetail

Dollery, B., Ho, C. M., & Alin, J. (2008). No lessons learned: A critique of the Queensland local government reform commission final report. *Agenda: A Journal of Policy Analysis and Reform, 15*(1), 67-84. https://www.researchgate.net/profile/Brian-Dollery-2/publication/228417457_No_Lessons_Learned_A_Critique_of_the_Queensland_Local_Government_Reform_Commission_Final_Report/links/0912f513676939386b000000/No-Lessons-Learned-A-Critique-of-the-Queensland-Local-Government-Reform-Commission-Final-Report.pdf

Dollery M. & Shah, A. (2020), *Local Public, Fiscal and Financial Governance: An International Perspective,* Palgrave McMillan.

Dollery, B., Kortt, M., & Grant, B. (2011). A normative model for local government de-amalgamation in Australia. *Australian Journal of Political Science, 46*(4), 601-615. https://doi.org/10.1080/10361146.2011.623670

Dollery, B., & Robotti, L. (Eds.). (2008). *The theory and practice of local government reform*. Edward Elgar Publishing.

Dollery, B. E. & Tiley, I. (Eds.) (2015). *Perspectives on Australian local government reform*, Federation Press.

Drew, J., & Dollery, B. (2014). The impact of metropolitan amalgamations in Sydney on municipal financial sustainability. *Public Money & Management, 34*(4), 281-288. https://doi.org/10.1080/09540962.2014.920201

Drew, J., & Dollery, B. (2014). Would bigger councils yield scale economies in the Greater Perth Metropolitan Region? A critique of the Metropolitan Local Government Review for Perth local government. *Australian Journal of Public Administration, 73*(1), 128-137. https://doi.org/10.1111/1467-8500.12059

Drew, J., & Dollery, B. (2014b). Separation anxiety: an empirical evaluation of the Australian Sunshine Coast Regional Council de-amalgamation. *Public Money & Management, 34*(3), 213-220. https://doi.org/10.1080/09540962.2014.908032

Drew, J., & Dollery, B. (2015). Breaking up is hard to do: the costs of de-amalgamation of the Delatite shire council. *Public Finance and Management, 15*(1), 1-23.ttps://link.gale.com/apps/doc/A406900174/AONE?u=anon~d422d281&sid=googleScholar&xid=900b45dc

Drew, J. & Dollery, B. E. (2021). *New South Wales State Government Failure? An Empirical Analysis of the Cootamundra Gundagai Regional Council Forced Merger*, unpublished paper, UNE Centre for Local Government, University of New England.

Drew, J., Kortt, M. A., & Dollery, B. E. (2016a). Did the big stick work? An empirical assessment of scale economies and the Queensland forced amalgamation program. *Local Government Studies, 42*(1), 1-14. https://doi.org/10.1080/03003930.2013.874341

Drew, J., Kortt, M. A., & Dollery, B. (2016b). No Aladdin's cave in New South Wales? Local government amalgamation, scale economies, and data envelopment analysis specification. *Administration & Society, 49*(10), 1450-1470. https://doi.org/10.1177%2F0095399715581045

Fahey, G., Drew, J., & Dollery, B. (2016). Merger myths: a functional analysis of scale economies in New South Wales local government. *Public Finance and Management, 16*(4), 362. https://www.proquest.com/openview/208d4de652 e10a22e4204203bcb4e827/1?pq-origsite=gscholar&cbl=44221

Fellows, C., Dollery, B. E. & Marques, R. (2021). *An Empirical Evaluation of the 2008 Queensland Compulsory Council Consolidation*, unpublished paper, UNE Centre for Local Government, University of New England.

Independent Local Government Review Panel (ILGRP) (2013, April). *Future Directions for NSW Local Government - Twenty Essential Steps*, ILGRP. https://tinyurl.com/yj77tkjc

Independent Local Government Review Panel (ILGRP). (2013). *Revitalizing Local Government*, ILGRP.

Local Government Association of Queensland (LGAQ) (2005). *Size, shape and sustainability of Queensland local government: Discussion paper*, LGAQ.

Local Government Association of Queensland (LGAQ) (2006), *Size, Shape and Sustainability: Guidelines Kit*, LGAQ.

Local Government Association of Queensland (LGAQ) (2007), *Submission to Local Government Reform Commission*, LGAQ.

Local Government Reform Commission (LGRC) (2007), *Report of the Local Government Reform Commission Vol. 1*, LGAQ.

McQuestin, D., Drew, J., & Dollery, B. (2017), Do municipal mergers improve technical efficiency? An empirical analysis of the 2008 Queensland municipal merger program, *Australian Journal of Public Administration, 77*(3), 442-455. https://doi.org/10.1111/1467-8500.12286

NSW Division of Local Government.(2012). Destination 2036 Action Plan, https://lgnsw.org.au/common/Uploaded%20files/Misc/Destination_2036_-_ Action_Plan.pdf.

TCorp. (2013. April). *Financial Sustainability of the New South Wales Local Government Sector*, 20. https://tinyurl.com/yhymt5h6

Vince, A. (1997). Amalgamations. In B. E. Dollery & N. A. Marshall (Eds.), *Australian Local Government: Reform and Renewal*, Macmillan, 51-171.

CASE STUDY 5

The Black Hole of 10BA

Justin Macdonnell

Stated simply, 10 BA was a hurried amendment to the Australian
Tax Act that permitted a 150% write-off to investors in the
local film industry and in the process made it one of the most
extravagant such benefits in the developed world. Aimed at
stimulating private investment in new film ventures, it quickly
became a rort and backfired. Announced as policy-on-the-run
for short-term political advantage in an election campaign, it
was enacted in panic and confusion and pursued doggedly at
considerable cost to revenue even after it was abundantly clear
that it had failed spectacularly in its objective. Not only did
the costs exceed the benefit, but the mechanism itself opened
the door to dubious characters and even more dubious practice
in the industry. A change of government was later to modify
10 BA to a more useful scale. Eventually, it was outmoded by
other, better focused support programs.

Infant industry

The central premise of this case study is not so much what 10
BA was or what it did but rather the mechanism it employed
and its implications for public arts policy-making. There's
little doubt that the re-emergence of the Australian film

industry in the 1960/70s arose from a mix of factors. Resurgent nationalism in the cultural domain was one. Forceful advocates to government, like Phillip Adams and Barry Jones, to the willing ear of an intrigued Prime Minister like John Gorton, were another. Above all, its success resulted from government intervention, especially financial. The initiatives of the Gorton and Whitlam governments had set the pace and in subsequent years film agencies had been established in all states.

Although the annual budgets of the state film corporations and the Australian Film Commission (AFC) combined could not have produced enough revenue for even one big Hollywood feature, they had willy nilly sustained an industry which produced upwards of 190 films over the decade to 1980. Dozens of directing talents had emerged achieving national and even some international recognition. But all was not well. A Peat Marwick Mitchell report commissioned by the AFC (1979) argued that the Australian market did not have the capacity either to absorb the current output or cover its costs. Some reform of the AFC followed, but how to generate sufficient investment remained the burning question. The simple fact was Australia was then a country of 17 million in an English-speaking world of 350 million of whom two thirds lived in the USA with its distinct entertainment preferences. Whatever way it was considered, the Australian film industry was boutique and 'Crocodile Dundee ' notwithstanding, likely to remain so.

Panic mode

Not unnaturally, private investors were reticent to put their money into such high-risk activity. Government funding for feature films was limited to just 65% of their agreed budgets. Somehow tax incentives had to be provided to encourage investment. In 1978 the Minister for Home Affairs, Bob Ellicott persuaded his colleagues to approve a provision under section 10B of the Tax Act by which money invested in films could be claimed as a tax deduction over the two years following the release of a film. Profits made by the film in this period were subtracted from the deduction. But the scheme failed to attract, and potential investors turned to alternative devices involving "gearing" i.e. a higher rating tax deduction for each dollar invested.

The government panicked and in 1980 announced a crackdown on "expenditure recruitment" or tax avoidance schemes, in particular disallowing tax benefits gained under such schemes. Then Treasurer, John Howard turned this into something of a crusade, even to pushing the notion of retrospective legislation to catch the perpetrators of the so-called "bottom of the harbour" schemes. The result called a halt to virtually all private film investment. The direct effects of this were immediately seen in the South Australian Film Corporation's decision at that time to abandon feature film making entirely.

Sensing that they had unwittingly perpetrated a "baby with the bathwater" trick, some weeks before the 1980 election Ellicott announced a new taxation scheme: a 150% write-off on film investment expenditure in the year of expenditure. That was big news! The government's over-reaction was the genesis of the now notorious 10BA provision which gave successive governments so many headaches both in its definition and in its management.

Thought up in the white heat of the campaign trail, it became one of the most generous allowances to any industry anywhere in the Western world. As such, it carried the seeds of its own undoing. Prime Minister, Malcolm Fraser later claimed at a dinner held in May 1981 (Dept. of P.M.&C., 1981) that it came about from a casual conversation with the make-up artist preparing him for a television commercial during the campaign.

He'd asked how business was faring and she unloaded about the terrible state of the industry and lack of work. She'd had 16 films cancelled. John Howard, in his keenness to stop the tax avoidance cheats, had caught up with a scheme which had been used quite successfully to fund Australian films. Fraser declared he would look into it (Dept. of P.M.&C, 1981). This ended in what might fairly be regarded as the plus ultra of the adage "it seemed like a good idea at the time". Apocryphal or not, it was as a result of something very like this that the government got itself into a huge mess.

Making it up

Accordingly, the stated aim of amending the Tax Act was to provide a deduction equal to 100% of capital expenditure on the acquisition of initial copyright in the new Australian film. It also provided for a tax exemption for an investor' s net earnings from any such film. The maximum tax exemption was an amount of 50% of the capital expenditure that qualified for 150% deduction. To be entitled to the deduction an investor had to become the first owner, or one of the first owners, of the copyright of a film which the Minister for Home Affairs certified to be eligible. To qualify this had to be a feature film, a documentary or miniseries or television drama. Run-of-the-mill productions like TV commercials, variety programs, sport or public events were ineligible.

Then came the tricky bit: a key provision was that the deduction would apply only to those films which represented a *genuine* loss. Accordingly, even if the film was certified eligible, if it made a profit the investors were not eligible for the deduction. During the election campaign the Treasurer stipulated that the deduction would be available only in the financial year in which the investor had expended the capital. He was also unwise enough to quote a figure of $2 million as an estimate of revenue likely to be forgone as a result of the initiative. Even more foolishly in March 1981, in answer to a question in Parliament, he confirmed that estimate. By April, in response to another question, he was forced to acknowledge that the lost revenue would be nearer to $30 million though the following day he amended that to $20 million. The fact was that no one knew what the true figure was and that became the nub of the ongoing mess.

Not surprisingly, there had been what the Treasurer mildly termed a "very strong response to the government's initiative" (Commonwealth, 1981, May 27, p. 2703) from those eager to invest. In reality, it was a stampede. To the end of 1981, 70 applications for certification as Australian films had been processed by the time the bill had been introduced to the Parliament. The total budgeted cost of these was $130 million and income tax deductions for 100% of that amount were obviously to be sought. Howard was left to observe: "unhappily there has been noted some intervention by elements whose only concern appears to be exploitation of the concession in an unacceptable way. Responsible film authorities have registered their concern about that" (Commonwealth, 1981, May 27, pp. 2703-2704). In other words, the carpetbaggers had arrived. Scores of these films never saw the light of a silver screen. It became a running joke and for the government a running sore.

The grifters

The film industry erupted claiming that what the scheme did was to deliver the industry's future even further into the hands of greater tax avoidance merchants than had previously been the case under the unamended clause 10B. Accordingly, the government backtracked deciding that, with effect from the commencement of the scheme on October 1, 1980, the deduction would be available only in the year in which the film had been completed and first exhibited. This change brought the new concessions into line with the existing income tax law but provided deductions over two years for the cost of acquiring a film copyright. In short, the government had made a precipitate, ill-thought-out announcement, introduced legislation which differed drastically from its original announcement and then proceeded to amend its own bill in the House by reverting to what it originally announced.

As Labor MP and noted film buff, Barry Jones observed: "this is the shonkiest piece of legislation that the government has introduced since this morning" (Commonwealth, 1981, June 3, p. 3720). The Treasurer tried to wriggle out of the debacle by saying first, that the originally estimated $2 million revenue forgone had been put together by the AFC and then, that while the information available to the government at the time the legislation was introduced indicated that about 170 films had been referred to the Department of Home affairs for certification, it was equally true that spokesmen for the film industry had declared that it was beyond the capacity of the industry to produce anything like that number in a year. This either missed or obscured the point of whether 10BA was still diverting financial resources from good into bad. The PM scarcely helped matters by his lugubrious account of the origins of the mess at the NIDA dinner only four days after the Bill had been introduced.

Not long after, the Treasurer was back on his feet explaining to the, by now, bewildered House what was actually going on. In answer to the Leader of the Opposition who asked if the total cost of the forgone revenue was now estimated at $120 million, he explained that the statement that he had made earlier meant that the people who made investments prior to the date the legislation was introduced would have them treated for tax purposes fully in the manner outlined in the statement made back in December previous year by the then Minister for Home Affairs (Ellicott having meanwhile moved on) and amendments to give effect to that announcement would be introduced to the Parliament the following day. He added that it was "a very generous concession" (Commonwealth, 1981, June 4, p. 3106). In fact, Howard, who even in those days was very much an economic "dry" within the Liberal Party, could not have been other than embarrassed by the whole affair. As the shadow Treasurer commented: "the Treasurer has... plainly been forced to carry the can for the Prime Minister's penchant for blatant electioneering. These concessions represent little more than outright pork barrelling" (Commonwealth, 1981, June 2, p. 3266).

To lose or not to lose, that is the question

To add a further level of contradiction, one should note that while all this was going on, the AFC's funding for 1981 was 40% less in real terms than it had been in 1975/76 (the last year of the Whitlam government) and despite the fact that the estimates of lost revenue under 10BA had ranged from $2 to $20 million, the Treasurer in his second reading speech had offered no costings at all. This was almost entirely unprecedented from a budgetary point of view, especially from a government otherwise arguing for tight fiscal policy.

Nevertheless, timing the write-off provision so that they would change to the year in which the film was *finished* had been a good move. The shadow Treasurer noted that this was not: "a major change for people genuinely interested in investing in film, but it was a blow for those people looking to make a quick tax dollar" (Commonwealth, 1981, June 5, p. 3267). Now, however, the Prime Minister had bowed to pressure from industry and stepped in again and the Treasurer had been forced to make a second humiliating change in the space of one week so that money invested between the date of the initial announcement and the introduction of the bill would be eligible for an immediate write-off, as originally proposed.

Among the issues canvassed were: that the legislation offered financial incentives for the production of large numbers of low quality films; that it was likely to act as a disincentive to the production of high quality films by forcing them to compete with tax avoidance films in securing the services of writers, producers, technicians and performers; that it would introduce destabilising factors into the economics not only of the film industry but also of related industries particularly advertising – costs of which had already risen sharply as a result of announcements made in 1980; that in aiming to extend tax incentives to films made under coproduction agreements with foreign companies, it would also increase pressure on available resources and skilled personnel; and finally, it would provide an enormous concealed subsidy to the (commercial) television industry. Jones observed: "The unfortunate Treasurer has had to adopt more positions than in the Kama Sutra in order to adapt itself to these changes" (Commonwealth, 1981, June 5, p. 3270).

Notwithstanding, the government responded that the flood of new money would create: "a greater opportunity of choice than ever before in the investors that genuine filmmakers would like" (Commonwealth, 1981, June 5, p. 3270). During the second reading speech in the Senate, Susan Ryan, Opposition spokesperson for the arts described the legislation as representing: "a saga of extravagant promises, broken promises, modified promises and the absolute chaos that has been created in the film industry by the government's handling of this issue is something that all Australians who are interested in having an Australian film industry or who are involved in the Australian film industry will not forget for a very long time" (Commonwealth, 1981, June 1, p. 3100).

Expenditure by stealth

Through all of this, the question remained as to why, if the Government was so willing to put taxpayers' money into the film industry, they would not do so by way of increasing assistance to the AFC which was after all the national body set up by the Whitlam government and maintained by the Fraser government to engage in investment in films and assist their production. "The present method", Ryan said was "public expenditure by stealth" (Commonwealth, 1981, June 1, p. 3100) for although it was a burden on the taxpayer it was a hidden burden, a disguised burden which allowed the government with its particular animus toward the public sector to claim that it was reducing the public expenditure when in reality it was creating a large and undefined new commitment on the public purse. She also argued for amendments that would have excluded from expenditure eligible for the concession those salaries paid to overseas talent and the brokerage fees, which by then had shot up to 20% of production costs under the influence of the newly announced incentives. In the event, the Government refused the first but accepted the second.

The legislation was eventually proclaimed in June of that year and shortly afterwards, during Senate Estimates Committee an official of the Department of Home Affairs acknowledged that up to that time they had received 251 applications specifically made under the legislation of which 123 had received provisional certificates and 2 final certificates. Provisional certificates amounted to $113 million or an average of just $1 million (Commonwealth Estimates, 1981, Sept. 15, p. 48). It was a measure of the behemoth which the Government had so unnecessarily created. The fact is that no one could at that stage accurately calculate the impact on wasted effort and talent represented by the scheme or more critically the amount of revenue forgone by Treasury.

Back from the brink

A change of government in 1983 brought yet more shifts in the 10BA saga. Early in the piece, the Hawke administration announced that it would amend the taxation incentives to eliminate the "bunching" of film production. The modification proposed that deductions would henceforth be available at the point of investment in a qualifying Australian film, provided films were completed within two years. The amendment would apply to investment in qualifying Australian films being made after January 1983. Clearly, the new Government was hoping that the statement made so early in its term would serve to allay concern in the film industry about whether the proposed amendments would proceed and, indeed, whether the Government was taking seriously the views it had expressed in Opposition.

The next big step came in the 1983/84 budget when the Treasurer, Paul Keating announced that tax concessions on capital expenditure would be reduced from 150% to 133% and exemption from income tax on film revenue reduced from 50% to 33%. Those who had benefited from the generous provisions in the past and even serious film producers were concerned at the changes. The Government was at pains to point out that it not been seeking to reduce its commitment to the film industry, but to establish a more commercially viable scene. "The government recognises that the bulk of investment in Australian films must come from the private sector, so that tax incentives, although reduced, are still generous enough to attract funds to the industry", the Arts Minister Barry Cohen stated (AFR, 1981).

Although reductions to the tax concessions were construed in some quarters as a slap in the face for producers, it was in fact a move toward more responsible costing and production standards within the industry generally. The AFC and the Government had both realised that the incidents which had occurred before each 30th of June – when previously unknown "producers" were hustling multi-million dollar deals for financing – could not go on indefinitely. They had also identified the surge in revenue to the accountants and lawyers who had benefited from the tax concessions – perhaps more than the industry itself. The AFC estimated that the reduction in tax concessions would mean that the breakeven point for private investment had increased from $.24 in the dollar to $.30 in the dollar.

Meanwhile, the Film and Television Production Association of Australia had issued a statement claiming that: "the film industry is aghast of the government's broken promises. This breach of promise will virtually eliminate investment in an industry which is struggling to re-establish itself after two years of upheaval brought about by inadequate legislation" (AFR, 1981). Which does go to demonstrate, if it needed demonstrating, that in some industries you cannot please any of the people any of the time.

Cohen did some waffling about the government having taken steps which it considered would lead to a greater concentration of creative and other resources on high-quality films with general prospects for commercial success: "In assessing the effectiveness of the [previous] deductions , the government has become concerned that they have created conditions whereby an increasing number of films of doubtful merit are being promoted to the public by commission agents who neither understand the industry nor have its best interest at heart. I am informed that film proposals to the value of $200 million were actively promoted to the public during June last year. There is no doubt that very many of these proposals were without fundamental merit..." (Commonwealth, 1981, August 24, p. 183).

New lamps for old

One of the government's moves in the 1983/4 budget was to allocate $5 million to the AFC to spend directly on productions of film and television projects, proved to be highly successful. The Commission chose a wide range of productions from outright commercial efforts to artistic gambles and offered them a range of assistance options. That proved so worthwhile that in 1984/85 the federal budget provided for a further $5 million although the appropriation was referred to as the second and final payment in the government scheme. It was thought that Treasury was keen to restrict the operation of the fund to whatever revenue it generated itself from the $10 million received. That was classic direct subvention policy. Later, during the 1984 election campaign, the Prime Minister promised twice that the film tax concessions under section 10 BA would remain for the life of the forthcoming Parliament that was, in effect, until 1987. By that time the industry came to recognise that the maintenance of a 133% tax write-off together with the AFC production fund provided a good balance and largely lobbied for its retention.

The argument against 10BA had always been that tax revenue forgone was an undesirable way of providing public sector assistance to any industry though the contrary argument was also put namely that there was, in fact, little or no net loss to government revenue from film tax concessions. To the contrary, it was alleged that as filmmaking is a very labour-intensive industry, money recouped by subsequent income tax, payroll tax, sales and company tax derived from film production balanced this out. There were also not insignificant overseas earnings, particularly in US dollars and primarily from television which contributed to the balance of funds.

At the same time, the real fiscal position had started to clarify. Official estimates of revenue forgone through the film tax concessions between 1981 and 1984 was $90 million. This was not, of course, the whole picture. Treasury calculated that in 1981 there had been negligible unspecified loss to revenue through the concessions which were made retrospective to October 1980. In 1981/82 the lost revenue was estimated at $13 million, in 1982/83 at $28 million and in 1983/84 $40 million. On the other hand, the industry – both producers and government film agencies - believed those figures exaggerated the loss. For instance, the calculations did not assume that investment would have gone if not to film then some other tax shelter or that the investment would necessarily have been tax-deductible. They were simply the total amounts of the deduction against income, taking account also of the tax-free nature of the film's first revenue dollars.

Building a bank

For four years rumours have been rife about threats to 10BA until, towards the end of Cohen's time as Minister, a new scenario was being unveiled by the AFC to create an Australian Film Loan Corporation on the lines of the Australian Industry Development Corporation. If this did not exactly bring things back to Gorton and the Australian Film Development Corporation in 1970, it came interestingly close. In November 1986 the AFC produced a discussion paper in which it advocated the development of a package of assistance measures aimed at putting the industry on the stable financial footing. The impetus of the paper came from the 1985 general debate on tax, increasing pressure to eliminate tax shelters such as division 10BA. In addition, the AFC was concerned by the sharply diminished film fundraising following the reduction of the 10BA concession and the planned reductions from July 1987 of marginal tax rates. These were expected to push the free-sale benchmark to around 80% of production costs, a figure beyond the reach of many if not most theatrical films and most though not all television product.

We should go back and remember that when first proposed, the 10BA legislation was defended in the face of scepticism and concern, as a model of government intervention. The expectation was it would create an orderly capital market for film ventures and eventually so it proved for the most part. An AFC report of the time notes: "as a device for recruiting private investment legislation was highly effective. The cap-in-hand financing tactics of the 1970s gave way to the less gruelling rigours of private and public offers" (AFC, 1986). But that is true only after the tax write-off was modified by reducing it from 150% to 133%.

As well, a concomitant of this brave new world was still the issue of taxation revenue lost. Original estimates, as we have seen, varied wildly from the understated $2 million to the seemingly grossly inflated $30 million. The fact is there had been little way of knowing. The AFC report goes on: "figures later supplied by Treasury showed that by 1982/83 the costs had reached $60 million and by 1983/84 $100 million. The escalation prompted a review of the legislation whose outcome was announced in August 1980 and was a decision to reduce the tax benefit. However, the reduction had no discernible effect. Investment continued its upward trajectory. The peak was reached in 1984/85 when investment topped $185 million and the cost to revenue nudged $155 million. Against this background, the government announced a second change as part of a package of tax reform measures. The reduction led to a downturn in investment in 1985/86 to $159 million although the impact was mitigated by transitional arrangements. A further downturn is expected in 1986/87" (AFC, 1986, p. 4).

The final countdown

These two reductions altered in a quite dramatic way the whole equation of investment in the film industry. When it was first introduced, the 10BA legislation provided investors with an effective 90% subsidy. The first modification of that generous provision which occurred in 1983 reduced this to 80% and the second in September 1985 to 60%. From July 1987 the effect of subsidy would be 40% reflecting the reduction in marginal tax rates. This was a significant drop and when it happened Division 10BA was no longer of use to film producers and the AFC had had to come up with an entirely new means of financing. Not surprisingly, the idea which attracted most attention was that of the loan fund, but it was not until July 1988 that the Film Finance Corporation, a wholly owned Commonwealth company with funds of $70 million was finally proclaimed. The AFC remained in its developmental and supervisory role with a direct small grant-giving function and with a three-year commitment of $6 million per year. 10 BA was amended to allow an immediate 100 % write-off with all film revenue taxed thereafter.

Here, as with so many arts and arts-related initiatives in Australia, the wheel had come full circle. Not only had it swung back towards the much earlier Gorton era Film Development Corporation model, but also to the notion, dear to Treasury's heart, that direct subvention was to be preferred to tax forgone, the principle being that by quantifying grants, subvention reveals the extent of a government's commitment to whatever the cause.

Conclusion

So, in a moment of electoral stress a government that understood little of the dynamics of film making but wanted to be able to offer good news to the electorate, abandoned its characteristic fiscal prudence and went overboard. There is a paradox here: the Liberal Party's philosophy has always been to prefer private investment over public expenditure. But by amending the tax act to an absurdly generous degree it did the very opposite of what it intended and allowed an imagined, short-term political gain to outweigh ordered thinking and public policy. It permitted adventurers who had no interest in the industry or in ever seeing a film completed, to use the mechanism to their own narrow advantage. There was no plan to deal with that. Attempts to explain it and in time to modify it only served to make the problem worse. At its height the government was incapable of quantifying the cost but more than that it wasted money that might have been channelled directly to its own film agency or to legitimate producers. It was risible and lampooned at the time which in itself damaged the industry it sought to assist. Eventually, a balance was struck between direct and indirect support of the industry which with greater forethought and better evaluation could have been achieved from the beginning. But as has been said: all strategy is lost in the heat of battle.

References

Australian Film Commission, (1979). *Towards a more effective Commission: the AFC in the 80's.* Peat, Marwick, Mitchell Services

Australian Film Commission. (1986). *Film assistance: future options.* Allen and Unwin.

Australian Financial Review (1981, August 26). *Interview with Commonwealth Arts Minister, Barry Cohen.*

Commonwealth, *Estimates Committee*, Senate, 13-15 Sept., 1981(Austl.). p 48.

Commonwealth, *Parliamentary Debates*, House of Representatives, 27 May, 1981, Malcom Fraser, Prime Minister) (Austl.).

Commonwealth, *Parliamentary Debates*, House of Representatives, 3 June, 1981, Treasurer (Austl.).

Commonwealth, *Parliamentary Debates*, House of Representatives, 4 June, 1981. (Austl.).

Commonwealth, *Parliamentary Debates*, House of Representatives, 5 June, 1981. (Austl.).

Commonwealth, *Parliamentary Debates*, House of Representatives, 24 June, 1983. (Austl.).

Department of Prime Minister & Cabinet (1981, May 31). *Address to the National Institute of Dramatic Arts.* Prime Minister of Australia (Press release). .https://pmtranscripts.pmc.gov.au/sites/default/files/original/00005598.pdf

CASE STUDY 6

The $6.2 million Payroll System that cost Queensland $1.25 billion

Henrico Dolfing

The payroll system implementation disaster at Queensland Health in 2010 is said to be the most spectacular technology project failure in the Southern Hemisphere and arguably the second worst failure of public administration in Australia's history. The handling of the fires this year being first. It also easily fits the bill of being called a 'White Elephant Project' with its startling cost over-runs and ongoing failures to accurately deliver its intended services.

Queensland Health is the public sector healthcare provider for Queensland, providing dental, medical, and aged-care facilities in Queensland, which has the most geographically dispersed population of all Australian states. Queensland Health needs to ensure that adequate healthcare services can be provided in the most remote parts of the state, which has a population of 5.07 million across an area of 1.85 million square kilometres. Every day, the organization provides hospital services to approximately 40,000 people and is responsible for approximately 85,000 employees across 300 sites.

What began as an $6.19 million contract between the State of

Queensland and IBM Australia to replace Queensland Health's aging payroll system eventually led to over 35,000 payroll mistakes and will ultimately cost taxpayers a whopping $1.25 billion. When the system went live, a large number of Queensland Health employees, including doctors and nurses, were either incorrectly paid or not paid at all. It led to the resignation of the minister of health, industrial strike action and loss of staff members to other employers.

Timeline of Events

2002

At this point in time Queensland Health used two systems for their payroll: Lattice and the Environment for Scheduling Personnel (ESP) rostering engine. Lattice and ESP were rolled out progressively over six years from 1996 to 2002. Payroll departments were part of their respective districts. Processing of pay was undertaken locally and there were close working relationships between line managers and local payroll staff. Whilst processing of pay occurred locally, the actual running of the pay was undertaken centrally; essentially, a 'hub and spoke' model was used. Lattice required a substantial amount of manual interventions to accommodate the complex award and incentive structures within Queensland Health.

2003

In 2003 the Queensland State government formally established a government shared services initiative (SSI) mandating that all state government departments, including Queensland Health, replace their existing legacy payroll systems with a standardized software solution that incorporates SAP HR and SAP Finance (SAP, or Systems Applications and Products, is a widely-used enterprise resource planning (ERP) software). The overarching objective of the SSI was to consolidate technology and resources through delivering a high-quality solution with standardized business processes.

The SSI was expected to deliver the following benefits: (1) increased opportunities through enabling workforce mobility; (2) increased visibility into the cost of services; (3) reduced data duplication through the consolidation of systems; (4) reduction in costs associated with licensing agreements; (5) reduction of personnel; (6) achieve economies of scale; (7) enable the government organizations to focus on their core competencies, thus increasing the standard of service; and (8) consistency of HR and finance information across all government agencies.

2005

In 2005, just three years after the progressive rollout was completed, Queensland Health received notification from the Lattice system vendor, Talent2, that their existing Lattice system was becoming obsolete and was no longer going to be supported, with services and updates ceasing on June 30, 2008. As a result, Queensland Health needed to consider replacing the obsolete Lattice system much sooner than it would have liked. SSI decided that the system for payroll would be SAP ECCS and Workbrain (Workbrain is an employee self-service kiosk providing web-based workforce management solutions for large enterprises). Accordingly, it was decided that Queensland Health would replace the Lattice I ESP system with SAP ECC5 I Workbrain as part of the shared services initiative.

2007

As part of the SSI, the Queensland government established CorpTech within the Queensland Treasury to oversee the standardized implementation across all state government departments. CorpTech was responsible for overseeing the consultant selection process (Request for Information, Request for Proposals, and Invitation to Offer) and managing the consulting organizations. CorpTech sent out a Request for Information (RFI) on July 2, 2007, and four consulting firms responded: Accenture, IBM, Logica, and SAP. Afterwards, CorpTech requested detailed proposals from these firms on July 25, 2007.

Prior to the RFI being issued, CorpTech had managed the implementation of SAP HR at the Department of Housing, and SAP Finance at the Department of Justice. These implementations proved to be quite costly as a substantial number of consulting firms and private consultants had been utilized. Due to the large expense associated with the multiple consulting firms, the consultant methodology for the SSI was changed to the prime contractor model on August 16, 2007. Subsequently, on September 12, 2007, CorpTech released an Invitation to Offer, and IBM, Accenture, and Logica responded. Ultimately, on December 5, 2007, IBM officially signed an $98 million contract to be the prime contractor of the SSI.

2008

Around October 2008, IBM had not achieved any of the "contracted performance criteria." It had, however, had been paid $32 million of its AU$98 million contract. The idea to build a payroll system across the entire Queensland public service was now officially scrapped, but the decision was made to push ahead with a payroll system for Queensland Health.

2009

To cater for Queensland Health's specific business needs, including the complex award structure, retrospectivity, and concurrent employment, a significant number of customizations were made to both Workbrain and SAP.

Payroll and user acceptance testing were performed in parallel over a series of stages starting July 2009. The first test of the payroll compared the pays of only 10 percent of employees from all employee groups when performed in the SAP HR and Workbrain rostering solution as opposed to the legacy Lattice system, which resulted in an $1.2 million discrepancy in the biweekly payroll.

2010

A second payroll test occurred in February 2010, which only resulted in an $30,000 discrepancy; however, casuals and overtime claims were not tested. Queensland Health accepted the inherent risks and opted to go-live without full testing of all the functionalities of the system. IBM continued to operate under varying scope and the state government kept signing off on the change requests. The project documentation reveals that prior to the payroll system going live, the project underwent four revised go-live dates and four separate stages of change requests, often done at the last minute. By the time the system finally went live in March of 2010, 20 months after the original start date, the bill had already ballooned to $101 million. Given the significant issues identified following the initial go-live, it was decided to establish a payroll stabilization project specifically focused on stabilizing the new payroll system. The four key focus areas for this project were: standardization and improvement of district and division business processes; payroll processing; payroll system performance; and support and communications for staff, line managers, and other key stakeholders.

2012

The cost of going live with a premature system resulted in more than 35,000 payroll mistakes, and by this point it had cost the state in excess of $400 million just to operate the system. KPMG (2012) estimated that the cost of making the system function for the next five years would be another $836 million. Staff unrest was very high and this continued for some years. Current Queensland Health staff still report a lack of confidence in their payslips.

2013

IBM should never have been appointed as the prime contractor in Queensland's failed health payroll project, according to the findings of the Commission of Inquiry (Qld. Health, 2013) that investigated the bungled project. The inquiry, which ran for nearly three months at a cost of $5 million, heard from some 50 witnesses, including former premier Anna Bligh, former health minister Paul Lucas, and senior IBM executive Bill Doak. The report, by Commissioner Richard Chesterman, was handed down on July 31 in the Queensland Parliament by Premier Campbell Newman. Premier Newman described the project as "arguably the worst failure of public administration in Australia's history." The report was particularly damning of the procurement process that led to the appointment of IBM, and decisions made by senior public servants and contractors involved with the project. The report also found the state government could not recover any funds from IBM for the failure of the project, and that the decision to reach a negotiated settlement with IBM rather than commencing legal proceedings was made without any proper analysis.

2016

The Queensland government was ordered to pay significant costs to IBM Australia after failing in a bid to recoup losses from the health payroll debacle. The Newman government launched legal action against IBM in 2013, arguing the company had misrepresented its capability to deliver a new payroll system on time and on budget. But IBM challenged the lawsuit and pointed to a 2010 agreement that the company said released it from the damages claim. A trial was held in the Brisbane Supreme Court in 2016 with Justice Glenn Martin ruling in favour of IBM.

What Went Wrong

System availability

During the payroll cut-over period to the new system, there were significant issues with the availability of the system to payroll staff which reduced the processing time available. This created an initial backlog of payroll forms and unprocessed adjustments for the period just prior to the go-live date that grew over subsequent pay periods. It took approximately eight months to process the backlog of pay adjustments and forms to return to previous business as usual (BAU) levels.

Performance issues

The degree of retrospectivity accommodated by the Queensland Health payroll system, whereby staff could submit forms for work completed up to six years ago, was creating significant payroll system performance issues. Additionally, the various awards and entitlement programs within Queensland Health had become so complex with some payslips covering multiple pages.

System issues

As of 2 May 2012, there were 570 logged system issues, 76 of which were identified as having the potential to impact on staff pay. System defect fixes and enhancements were required to occur during designated 'major release' schedules, of which there were three scheduled per annum. There were some delays in addressing specific defects and issues due to the prioritization of other 'fixes' including the pay date change, changes associated with enterprise bargaining changes, legislative compliance changes, etc. There was a need to gain endorsement for an agreed longer-term approach to implementing key system changes so that the release windows could be utilized more effectively.

Overpayments and entitlements

As of May 2012, Queensland Health had overpaid staff $112.3 million, of which $16.5 million had been repaid and $3.3 million was waived, leaving $9 million outstanding. Queensland Health had an obligation under the Financial Accountability Act 2009 to recover these amounts; however, there was a moratorium in place preventing Queensland Health implementing overpayment recovery. Queensland Health was required to fund fringe benefit tax (FBT) liabilities associated with overpayments, and this represented a significant additional cost burden to Queensland Health. While the previously agreed overpayment moratorium was in place, the amount increased by approximately $1.7 million every two weeks. In addition to overpayments, the issue of employee leave and balances requires further investigation and analysis. Price Waterhouse Cooper has conducted a number of reviews into leave balances and they have identified that up to 20,000 leave transactions are still outstanding since the move from the previous Lattice Payroll system across to SAP.

New business processes

Part of the implementation of the new system was further standardization and centralization of payroll processing, including the introduction of central processing teams and a centralized pay run. As such, the key linkage between the districts and their local payroll providers was severed — payroll staff were required to process unfamiliar rosters for staff members across the state. In addition, fundamental differences in how districts and line managers were providing pay information and rosters were identified, with each district continuing to provide the information in the format they had developed locally (this was a continuation of what had occurred with the Lattice system; however, now the payroll officers responsible for interpreting the pay information from the districts did not have the local knowledge or relationships that had previously assisted with the interpretation process).

How Queensland Health Could Have Done Things Differently

The key findings from the Commission of Inquiry's report were as follows:

Project governance

Project governance prior to go-live, including managing relationships with key stakeholders, was not effective in ensuring roles and responsibilities were clearly articulated and in ensuring there was clear accountability for efficient and effective implementation of the system.

The governance structure for the system implementation, as it related to CorpTech, the prime contractor, and Queensland Health, was not clear, causing confusion over the roles and responsibilities of the various parties.

Management of the project became even muddier after it commenced. Numerous agencies and boards divided oversight and authority, causing significant confusion which, in the end, rendered them all "ineffective in establishing a shared understanding of stakeholder expectations in relation to the quality of project deliverables":

- The Solution Design Authority (SDA) (which, during this period, transformed into the program delivery office (PDO) of the state's CorpTech IT division);

- The Queensland Health Enterprise Solution Transition (Queensland HealthEST), the state's information technology management program and acting project manager (which inexplicably retitled the "Interim Solution" as the "Queensland

Health Implementation of Continuity" (Queensland HealthIC)
— no confusion there!);

- The executive steering committee (ESC), which included personnel from CorpTech as well as the shared services agency (SSA) and the Department of Education, Training and the Arts (DETA), and

- The "Release Steering Committee," which answered to both the ESC and CorpTech and counselled its chair regarding the development of the Interim Solution.

While there appeared to be lots of oversight of the program, Australia's auditor-general reported that "it was not clear which Accountable Officer had responsibility for the overall governance and successful completion of the whole project."

Scope and requirements

There was inadequate documentation of business requirements at the commencement of the project. The absence of a periodic review of the business needs contributed to subsequent difficulties with system testing and the implementation of a system which did not meet the needs of Queensland Health's operating environment. The complexity of the project was immense and involved the management of over 24,000 differing combinations of wage payments and withholdings for over 80,000 workers and subcontractors spread over 13 contractors and multiple industrial agreements. Because of the fear that the existing system was in imminent danger of immediate failure, IBM agreed to take just seven months to develop and implement an "Interim Solution" to tide the agency over until a full replacement became operational. Within that seven months, only two weeks were set aside at the beginning of the project to scope out the "critical business requirements" needed by the agency and the digital solutions that would respond to those demands. Not surprisingly, the lack of identifiable objectives was a significant cause of the project's abject bungling.

Go-live decision

When the system went live it was seriously deficient, causing staff not to be paid, or to be paid inaccurately. Neither party could have been under any misunderstanding that this was the inevitable result. It was obvious well before go-live that the project had been inadequately scoped.

> "When it went live it was seriously deficient, causing very many QH staff not to be paid, or to be paid inaccurately. Neither party could have been under any misunderstanding that this was the inevitable result. It was obvious well before Go Live that the Project had been inadequately scoped. Testing (especially UAT) revealed thousands of defects, a large percentage of which concerned functional aspects of the system. A competent and experienced tester (Mr Cowan) did precisely what his role called for in advising the customer (as the party deciding whether to accept the system) of these very major problems. Despite these warnings (ones which Dr Manfield said were the clearest sign he had seen of a system in distress) the State decided to Go Live" (Queensland Health Payroll System Commission of Inquiry Report, 2013).

> "There could have been no clearer warning of the functional deficiencies in the system and the real risk of there being defects beyond the very large number which Mr Cowan had to that date detected. Had there been any doubt up until this point, Mr Cowan's Final UAT Report put the matter beyond doubt. One does not need to have any technical knowledge to take from that report a very clear warning that, if the system proceeded to Go Live in its then state, there was a real likelihood, indeed perhaps an inevitability, that it would contain defects of a functional kind." Queensland Health Payroll System Commission of Inquiry Report. (Qld. Health, 2013).

Business processes

A number of critical business readiness activities and practices were not fully developed prior to the implementation of the new system. Several changes to payroll administration practices including the reallocation of processing duties within payroll were introduced at the same time as the release of the SAP and Workbrain systems.

Standardization

The implemented Workbrain (1,029 customizations) and SAP (1,507 customizations) systems were heavily customized and are not operating optimally in the Queensland Health environment. Customizations are costly to manage, increase risk and impact on system performance and should be minimized where practical.

Supplier

Despite its affiliation with a global digital leader, this was IBM Australia's first attempt at delivering a project of this size. That fact was not helpful considering that Queensland Health was probably the most complex of the Australian agencies needing the overhaul and was perhaps not the best candidate for IBM's first go.

Layer on top of those contributors the reality that the "Solution Design Authority," the state agency with the responsibility to define and maintain the scope, architecture, and design of the new system, was "passive, perhaps lazy" about communicating its requirements for a payroll system. Before project development began, the Solution Design Authority accepted IBM's "incomplete, ... unsatisfactory scope [of work] documents" as-is and with no questions (Qld. Health, 2013). The project was off to a horrible start.

Closing Thoughts

As a consequence of Queensland Health's disastrous payroll implementation project, the Queensland Government changed their Information Technology (IT) strategy and governance procedures.

Furthermore, the Queensland Government IT audit specified a series of constraints that must be placed on high-risk projects, which include the following:

1) project management personnel must be of the highest quality;

2) rigorous application of the Queensland Government project and program methodology;

3) the project must be approved by numerous chains of command, and

4) a reporting regime is to be established to increase the visibility of the costs associated with IT projects.

Being a state government department in the healthcare industry, Queensland Health is by definition already riddled with substantial layers of bureaucracy, adding to the complexity and increasing the difficulties associated with decision making, visibility, and accountability.

And these reforms, whilst necessary, add additional layers to the governance process, increasing both the number of bureaucratic decisions and the degree of red tape.

Consequently, both client and consultant organizations have been more cautious throughout recent technology projects in the public sector due to the increase in compliance which leads to project delays, and increased project costs.

Thus, aside from the financial and societal implications associated with the Queensland Health payroll implementation failure, the failure has also had national, industry-wide ramifications.

But do we really learn from these massive failures? Looking

at the long list of big technology projects gone wrong after this one, I doubt it.

Especially in the area of public services.

References

KPMG. (2012, May 31). *Review of the Queensland Health Payroll System.* https://drive.google.com/file/d/1CYkU94RXKmip0JNRnOFx8k3zZrU-57C1/view

Manongdo, R. (2014). *Queensland Health Payroll system – A case study on business process management and application enterprise integration.* Macquarie University https://drive.google.com/file/d/1roMN7qEiC-hjuxrDHG1FdOwfmL5g-Lav/view

Queensland Health (2013, July 31). Queensland Health Payroll System Commission of Inquiry. https://drive.google.com/file/d/1ZxyWqK3xuF8Pb7OWhLYZv2dpoE6yyMce/view

Eden, R., & Sedera, D. (2014). The largest admitted IT project failure in the Southern Hemisphere: a teaching case. In *Proceedings of the 35th International Conference on Information Systems* (pp. 1-15). Association for Information Systems (AIS). https://drive.google.com/file/d/1p997XIJ_4bmDJ_BTty7wg5ptgyDto58S/view

CASE STUDY 7

Whatever Happened to COVIDSafe?

Steven Schwartz AM

Life is short, the Art long; opportunity fleeting, experiment treacherous, judgement difficult. Hippocrates

Everything is politics. Thomas Mann

In the May 2021 budget, the federal government announced a Digital Economy Strategy designed to transform Australia into an international IT powerhouse by 2030. Like all similar government announcements, the new strategy promises lots of new jobs and unlimited prosperity but, before we start celebrating, it is worthwhile examining the government's track record in extracting value from IT projects. The historical analysis can begin with this chapter, which describes an attempt to harness IT for the public's benefit. The project failed, but its short and unhappy history holds valuable lessons that (if applied) would improve future policymaking.

Background

On 4 January 2020, the World Health Organisation (WHO) used social media to call attention to a cluster of unusual pneumonia cases in Wuhan, China (WHO, 2020). Eight days later, Chinese scientists shared the genetic sequence of the disease responsible for these cases—a novel coronavirus. The next day, the same virus was detected in Thailand; the pandemic had begun.

On 25 January, only three weeks after WHO first identified the cluster of cases in Wuhan, Victorian health authorities revealed that a traveller from Wuhan had brought the virus to Australia. The federal government immediately sought to reassure a worried public. According to the Minister for Health, Greg Hunt, "Australia has world-class health systems with processes for the identification and treatment of cases, including isolation facilities in each state and territory" (Dept. of Health, 2020, Jan. 25).

For the next month, the minister's confidence seemed justified. China stopped all air traffic out of Wuhan but flights to Australia from other parts of China and the rest of the world continued (Prime Minister, 2020). The number of COVID-19 cases remained low, and there were no deaths. In March, however, the situation changed dramatically. Cases began to multiply, and so did fatalities. The Ruby Princess cruise ship fiasco, in which infected passengers were allowed to disembark into the community, led to dozens of deaths.

Minister Hunt's insouciance about Australia's health capabilities had proven unjustified. Despite numerous warnings over the years (McKay & Dvorak, 2020), the country was not adequately prepared to deal with the pandemic. Unable to rely on our "world-class" contact tracing and isolation systems to combat the virus, political leaders resorted to more drastic interventions. They halted movements across national and state borders and forced citizens to stay home.

Border closures, shuttered schools, and lockdowns have devastating economic, health, and social consequences. Recognising that efficient and effective contact tracing is infinitely preferable to shutting down the economy and imprisoning the population, the federal government commissioned the Digital Transformation Agency to oversee the creation of a smartphone app that would accelerate contact tracing by automatically identifying people who come in contact with someone suffering from COVID-19.

The app, called *COVIDSafe*, was launched on 27 April 2020. The Prime Minister said it would, "save lives and save livelihoods." He encouraged all members of the public to install the app on their smart phones:

> "The more people who download this important public health app, the safer they and their family will be, the safer their community will be and the sooner we can safely lift restrictions and get back to business and do the things we love." (Department of Health, 2020, April 27)

More than two years have passed since the Prime Minister launched *COVIDSafe*. In that time, the app uncovered 17 contacts not identified by other means. (Commonwealth, 2021) It is not clear how many of the 17 contacts tested positive for COVID-19. Social distancing and travel restrictions remain in place along with sporadic lockdowns and border closures. The remainder of this chapter is devoted to understanding why the app was unsuccessful and extracting lessons from the *COVIDSafe* saga that could improve future policy making.

COVIDSafe: purpose, performance, politics

In March 2020, with COVID-19 cases multiplying rapidly, Australia faced an urgent and pressing need for efficient contact tracing. Community-driven contact tracing using a smart phone app was being implemented in Singapore and it seemed reasonable to adopt similar technology in Australia. The initial *COVIDSafe* budget was $2 million (Department of Health, 2020, April 27). This is not a large expenditure by government standards, especially considering the app's potential (albeit unmeasured) health benefits. Given its logic, aims and budget, *COVIDSafe* was not born a white elephant. It earned white elephant status by an all-too-familiar combination of poor messaging, hype, and hubris.

How *COVIDSafe* is supposed to work

When a new COVID-19 case is uncovered, contact tracers seek to identify the person's recent contacts and advise them to self-isolate. By enabling smartphones to automatically record everyday encounters, *COVIDSafe* was intended to speed up the tracing and notification process.

Using Bluetooth wireless technology, *COVIDSafe* scans the vicinity for nearby devices that also have the app installed. When *COVIDSafe* detects a nearby phone running the app, it stores the date, time and the encrypted identity of the phone owner on both phones. To protect privacy, the app does not store the locations of encounters, and automatically deletes data after three weeks.

No unauthorised person can access the encrypted data, not even the phone's owner. Should a *COVIDSafe* user test positive for COVID-19, a state or territory health official must request the user's consent to access saved information. If the user grants access, health officials upload a list of contacts to the *National COVIDSafe Data Store*. Contact tracers examine the list and advise whose exposure lasted at least 15 minutes to get tested and isolate themselves. The anonymity of *COVIDSafe* data is preserved by law and the names of infected people are not made public.

The *COVIDSafe* rollout

The Prime Minister announced the *COVIDSafe* project on 14 April 2020. The government declared that the app would need to be installed on 40% of all smartphones before they could ease social distancing restrictions. This target did not have an evidence base, and the health department did not conduct any modelling (Sadler, 2020), but 40% was manifestly inadequate. Even if the app worked flawlessly, it would record fewer than half of all contacts because *COVIDSafe* would be absent from more than 50% of smartphones. As it turned out, despite an extensive media campaign to convince people to install the app to their phones, downloads never reached the 40% target, which was quietly abandoned.

One reason some people were reluctant to install the app was a concern about personal privacy. Some feared that the app would permit the government to monitor their movements. This fear was unjustified, but comments made by government officials stoked suspicion.

For example, three days after the Prime Minister's announced *COVIDSafe*, the ABC reported that Adjunct Professor Paul Kelly, the Commonwealth's Deputy Chief Medical Officer at the time, refused to rule out making the *COVIDSafe* mandatory on all smartphones. At the same time, the Prime Minister called voluntary downloading "Plan A," which implied that Plan B would compel people to install the app on their phones (ABC News Live Blog, 2020). The uproar was immediate. In an about-face, the Prime Minister ruled out compulsory downloading the very next day. Unfortunately, the reputational damage had been done. A week before *COVIDSafe* was available for downloading, clumsy messaging had already dissuaded some members of the public from downloading it (Gillezeau, 2020).

COVIDSafe was made available to the public on 26 April 2020. Not surprisingly, for an IT project completed during a pandemic, there were one or two minor glitches. Initially, there was some confusion between *COVIDSafe* and the pre-existing *Coronavirus Australia* app (a compilation of information about the pandemic). Despite privacy concerns, one million people downloaded *COVIDSafe* within 24 hours of its launch. In the next two weeks, that number grew to 4 million (Meixner, 2020). Downloads were halfway to the government's target of having the app installed on 40% of Australia's 20 million smartphones (Granwal, 2020).

The government rolled out *COVIDSafe* before finalising the regulations for the collection and use of its data. As a result, tracking information was not available to state and territory contact tracers. As a result, there were no reports of the app identifying contacts and saving lives. Interest began to wane, and the rate of downloads slowed. Still, by 14 May, *COVIDSafe* was installed on 5.7 million (28% of smartphones). It was around this time that reports began to circulate about app's poor performance on iPhones.

COVIDSafe and iPhones

When the government launched the app, the Minister for Government Services, Stuart Robert stated that, "To be effective, users should have the app running in the background when they are coming into contact with others. Your phone does not need to be unlocked for the app to work" (Department of Health, 2020, April 27).

It seems Mr Robert's statement was not true for iPhones (around half of all Australian smartphones). Data reported to the Senate Estimates Committee on 26 May 2020 indicated that *COVIDSafe* running on locked iPhones missed many close contacts (Commonwealth, 2021). Keeping an iPhone unlocked with *COVIDSafe* on the screen improved performance a little, but this quickly ran down phone batteries. These iPhone issues were not a complete surprise; similar problems plagued the Singapore app, which served as a model for *COVIDSafe*. Software upgrades gradually improved *COVIDSafe's* performance, but it remained less than ideal.

Apple and Google Offer an Alternative

iPhone problems, and the absence of any "good news" stories about the app's value to public health, caused the pace of *COVIDSafe* downloads to slow considerably. By the end of June, the number reached 6.4 million, around 30 per cent of all smartphones. Contact tracers had accessed the app 90 times without uncovering an exposure not previously identified. At the same time, suspicion about privacy safeguards began to re-surface. Other countries that developed apps faced similar operational and privacy issues. To deal with poor performance and assuage worries about privacy, Apple and Google decided to jointly create an "Exposure Notification System" that would work on both Android and iPhones while still maintaining strict privacy (Chugh, 2020).

Like *COVIDSafe*, the Apple/Google system uses Bluetooth to log encounters, but it is not a traditional app. The notification system is integrated into phone operating systems thereby avoiding *COVIDSafe's* performance issues. Apple and Google invited health authorities to design apps using their system. However, to ensure complete privacy, the Apple/Google system does not transmit data to health authorities who then contact people at risk. Instead, app users exposed to a person who tests positive for COVID-19 receive a warning message directly from the system itself. The phones hold all the data and do all the work.

Although the Apple/Google system does not help health officials identify people who have been exposed to COVID-19, it can warn those who have come into contact with infected individuals to get tested and isolate themselves.

Given its performance and privacy advantages, 47 countries, states, and regional authorities designed apps to work with the Apple/Google system (Exposure Notification, 2021) Australia refused. According to Nick Coatsworth, Deputy Chief Medical Officer at the time, Australia would "absolutely not" switch to the Apple/Google system because it "fundamentally changes the locus of control." He went on to say:

> "There's no way we're shifting to a platform that will take out the contact tracers. ... I have bought into the app and I continue to ... think it's a great platform. It will identify cases eventually that haven't been determined by the contact tracers." (Grubb, 2020)

Coatsworth's comments did not stimulate an avalanche of new users for COVIDSafe. No one cared whether he "bought into the app," everyone knew that *COVIDSafe* was not "great," and phrases like "the locus of control" further stoked fears about privacy. Although it would have been possible to provide a method by which people who were alerted by the Apple/Google system could voluntarily inform health authorities, the government never tried (Chugh, 2020).

"To err is human, to blame others is politics," said former US Vice-President Hubert Humphrey. So, no one was surprised in July 2020 when Minister Robert finally admitted that *COVIDSafe* was not "great" and proceeded to blame its problems on Apple and Google. According to Mr Robert, the companies should modify their notification framework to suit Australia's *COVIDSafe* app rather than the other way around (Barbaschow, 2020).

COVIDSafe enters the land of BAU

By August, *COVIDSafe* vanished from the news. Border closures, lockdowns and social isolation rules ensured that Australia had low numbers of COVID-19, so there were hardly any contacts for *COVIDSafe* to detect. Ministers stopped exhorting the public to download the app and by early 2021, around one-third of users erased it from their phones (Taylor, 2021).

COVIDSafe became invisible, but it did not die. The Digital transformation Agency is still spending money to host the app and store contact data (should they ever find any). They are also translating *COVIDSafe* into Turkish, Punjabi and other languages.

A year after the Prime Minister launched *COVIDSafe*, Randall Brugeaud, Chief Executive of the Digital Transformation Agency, appeared before the Senate Estimates Committee (Commonwealth, 2021). He revealed that the cost of developing the app exploded from its initial budget of $2 million to $5.8 million. According to Brugeaud the total cost of hosting, perfecting, and translating *COVIDSafe* from its inception to 31 January 2021, was "$6,745,322.31, inclusive of GST".

The app is only known to have ever uncovered 17 contacts of COVID-19 not already identified by other means. Thus, the cost per contact was $396,783.67. A cost-benefit analysis has not been made available by the government, but some members of the Senate Estimates Committee appeared to believe the expenditure was somewhat excessive (Commonwealth, 2021).

According to Brugeaud, *COVIDSafe* is now in "business as usual" (BAU) mode requiring only a "small" outlay of $100,000 per month (Commonwealth, 2021). There is also a budget provision of about $200,000 per month to allow for potential "improvements." It is not clear what benefits the public can expect to receive for a yearly expenditure of $1.2 to $3.6 million or when the government might finally abandon *COVIDSafe*.

What can we learn from *COVIDSafe*?

Faced with growing numbers of COVID-19 cases, government ministers saw *COVIDSafe* as a way of "saving lives and saving livelihoods." The road from good intentions to valuable outcomes is never smooth; in the app's case, the road was rutted with deep potholes—poor performance, clumsy communication, changing priorities, and a lack of accountability.

Poor performance

COVIDSafe did not work well on iPhones. One minister urged iPhone users to leave their phones unlocked with *COVIDSafe* running in the foreground. This improved performance a little, but few iPhone owners were comfortable with permanently unlocked phones. Many did not know what "unlocked" and "foreground" mean. Rather than admit the app did not work well, official communications downplayed *COVIDSafe's* technical problems and continued to exhort users to use their phones in uncustomary ways. The failure to consider the disconnection between what technocrats wanted and the phone habits of the general public, led to disillusionment, disdain and the dismissal.

Clumsy communication

Policy makers were aware from the outset that a contact tracing app would stimulate privacy concerns. For this reason, *COVIDSafe* was created to preserve privacy. A technical analysis of dozens of early deployed Android contact tracing apps from around the world rated *COVIDSafe* the most private (Hatamian et al., 2021). Still, people remained suspicious, and their fears were stoked by unconvincing messaging.

The first problem was the government's initial download target—40% of smartphones. Plucked from thin air, the target was not based on statistical modelling and it was clearly inadequate. The odds that someone you encounter would have the app on their phone would be less than 50-50.

The existence of a download target led some to conclude that installing the app might be mandatory if voluntary downloads fell short of 40%. The refusal to rule out compulsory downloading, references to voluntary downloading as "Plan A" and a failure to even consider switching to the Apple/Google exposure notification system reinforced the idea that privacy might not be guaranteed. These fears were exaggerated but not entirely unjustified. Despite promises of confidentiality, the Singapore police were found to access data provided by their contact tracing app, which was the model for *COVIDSafe* (Illmer, 2021). The Prime Minister's reference to "Plan A" were quickly jettisoned, as was the 40% target, but these about-faces just made sceptics even more suspicious. Even members of parliament refused to download it (Crellin, 2020).

Privacy concerns about *COVIDSafe* were rendered moot when QR-code check-in became ubiquitous. Under the QR system, governments collected more information on the movement of citizens than *COVIDSafe* could ever provide, and there was little resistance. The difference in response is that QR codes worked. They provided useful evidence to contact tracers whereas COVIDSafe is widely perceived as ineffective.

Changing priorities

COVIDSafe was conceived when the government's policy was to manage outbreaks of COVID-19 to avoid overwhelming health services. When the policy switched to the complete suppression of the virus, the probability of a phone running *COVIDSafe* detecting an encounter with a COVID-19 case fell close to zero. The simply were no cases to detect.

Lack of accountability

The 24-hour news cycle coupled with a social media landscape dominated by self-appointed experts on pandemics put huge pressure on our political leaders to get things done. Instead of consultation, consideration, and careful planning, ministers like the public to think of them as vigorous leaders. Thus, the Australian government runs like a daily newsroom, flitting from one issue to the next. To appear strong and decisive, ministers feel compelled to do or say something—anything—about every issue on every day.

In their frantic rush to respond to the latest headline, nothing is more valuable to politicians than a short memory (Paraphrase of JK Galbraith's quote: *Nothing is so admirable in politics as a short memory).* Unkept promises are easily forgotten, mistakes buried, and good money is thrown after bad rather than admit a project did not work out. Accountability is essentially unknown. Politicians may lose their jobs because of sexual or financial scandals, but never because of policy failures. Public servants may sometimes take the rap, but this rarely means being fired. Most of the time, those responsible for stuff ups are merely moved to another job (often at a higher level).

At this very moment, somewhere in the government, a white elephant is quietly germinating. When it makes its public debut, there will be a temporary uproar, and then we will move on. Until there is real accountability among ministers and public servants, Australia's white elephant population will remain safely unendangered.

On 10 August 2022, the newly elected Labor government decommissioned the CovidSafe app. At a final cost of $21 million it identified only 17 cases. CovidSafe's status as a White Elephant is assured.

References

ABC News Live Blog. (2020, April 17). Deputy Chief Medical Officer doesn't rule out forcing Australians to download the Government's coronavirus tracing app. ABC News: Live Blog. Retrieved May 6, 2021, from https://www.abc.net.au/news/2020-04-17/paul-kelly-coronavirus-tracing-app/12158854

Barbaschow, A. (2022, July 22.). Minister still blaming COVIDSafe flaws on Apple and Google. ZDNet. Retrieved May 6, 2021, from https://www.zdnet.com/article/minister-still-blaming-covidsafe-flaws-on-apple-and-google/

Chugh, R. (2020, July 1). By persisting with COVIDSafe, Australia risks missing out on globally trusted contact tracing. The Conversation. Retrieved May 6, 2021, from https://theconversation.com/by-persisting-with-covidsafe-australia-risks-missing-out-on-globally-trusted-contact-tracing-141369

Commonwealth. Senate Community Affairs Legislation Committee Estimates (Public). 25 March 2021 (Australia). https://parlinfo.aph.gov.au/parlInfo/download/committees/estimate/22c34e3c-d8ac-47c2-9bb3-787f23065247/toc_pdf/Community%20Affairs%20Legislation%20Committee_2021_03_25_8630.pdf;fileType=application%2Fpdf#search=%22community%20affairs%22

Crellin, Z. (2020, May 11). We Asked Every MP And Senator Whether They Downloaded COVIDSafe And Here's What They Said. Pedestrian. Retrieved May 6, 2021, from https://www.pedestrian.tv/news/which-politicians-mps-senators-downloaded-covidsafe/

Department of Health. (2020, January 25). First confirmed case of novel coronavirus in Australia. [Press release]. Retrieved May 6, 2021, from https://www.health.gov.au/ministers/the-hon-greg-hunt-mp/media/first-confirmed-case-of-novel-coronavirus-in-australia

Department of Health. (2020, April 27). COVIDSafe: New app to slow the spread of the coronavirus. (Australia). Retrieved May 6, 2021, from https://www.health.gov.au/ministers/the-hon-greg-hunt-mp/media/covidsafe-new-app-to-slow-the-spread-of-the-coronavirus

Exposure Notification. (2021, May 3). In Wikipedia. Retrieved May 6, 2021, from https://en.wikipedia.org/wiki/Exposure_Notification

Gillezeau, N. (2020, April 17). COVID-19 Contact Tracing App. I get it but I don't like it. Financial Review. Retrieved May 6, 2021, from https://www.afr.com/technology/covid-19-contact-tracing-app-i-get-it-but-i-don-t-like-it-20200417-p54kqk

Granwal, L. (2020, Oct 8). Number of smartphone users in Australia in 2017 with a forecast until 2025. Statista. Retrieved May 6, 2021, from https://www.statista.com/statistics/467753/forecast-of-smartphone-users-in-australia/

Grubb, B. (2020, June 29). There is no way we're shifting: Australia rules out Apple/Google coronavirus tracing method. Sydney Morning Herald. Retrieved May 6, 2021, from https://www.smh.com.au/technology/there-s-no-way-we-re-shifting-australia-rules-out-apple-google-coronavirus-tracing-method-20200629-p5573s.html

Hatamian, M., Wairimu, S., Momen, N. et al. (2021, March 19). A privacy and security analysis of early-deployed COVID-19 contact tracing Android apps. Empirical Software Engineering, 26, 36 (2021). Retrieved May 6, 2021, from https://doi.org/10.1007/s10664-020-09934-4

Illmer, A. (2021, January 5). Singapore reveals Covid privacy data available to police. BBC News. Retrieved May 6, 2021, from https://www.bbc.com/news/world-asia-55541001

McKay, B., & Dvorak, P. (2020, August 13). A deadly coronavirus was inevitable. Why was no one ready? Wall Street Journal. Retrieved May 6, 2021, from https://www.wsj.com/articles/a-deadly-coronavirus-was-inevitable-why-was-no-one-ready-for-covid-11597325213

Meixner, S. (2020, June 2). How many people have downloaded the COVIDSafe app and how central has it been to Australia's coronavirus response? ABC News: Live Blog. Retrieved May 6, 2021, from https://www.abc.net.au/news/2020-06-02/coronavirus-covid19-covidsafe-app-how-many-downloads-greg-hunt/12295130

Prime Minister of Australia. (2020, March 19). Border restrictions. (Press release.) Retrieved May 6, 2021, from https://www.pm.gov.au/media/border-restrictions

Sadler, D (2020, May 6). No modelling on 40% trace target: health. Innovation Australia. Retrieved May 6, 2021, from https://www.innovationaus.com/no-modelling-on-40-trace-target-health/

Taylor, J. (2021, January 14). One-third of users have not updated the COVIDSafe app. The Guardian. Retrieved May 6, 2021, from https://www.theguardian.com/technology/2021/jan/14/one-third-of-australian-users-have-not-updated-covidsafe-app

World Health Organisation. (2020, May 27). Who Timeline COVID-19 [Press release]. Retrieved May 6, 2021, from https://www.who.int/news/item/27-04-2020-who-timeline---covid-19

CASE STUDY 8

Movie sets and racetracks – fates awaiting airports that aren't wanted. Beware an excess of optimism!

Paul Hooper

Why study failed airport projects?

The Suez Canal cost more than twice as much to build as was originally budgeted, its construction was delayed, it was not navigable by sailing ships, the volume of traffic initially fell below forecast levels, and the promoter ran into financial difficulties. An independent observer in 1867 might well have described the Suez Canal as a "white elephant".

This case illustrates that major infrastructure projects add capacity in large, lumpy units - half a canal was not an option. It also can take many years before demand begins to look respectable. Possibly, it might have been better to delay construction - after all, one of the most basic issues is "when is the best time to do this?". But even this question is problematic. The experience with building ports and railways has been that transport infrastructure results in economic development, and this development generates the business required to support the venture.

This argument continues to be used today to, at least in part, justify transport projects. An alternative view favoured by many economists is that actual demand should precede an increase in supply/capacity. The existence of failed airport projects motivated by the argument "build it and the customers will come" perhaps casts doubt on the ability of transport infrastructure projects to produce demand out of thin air. Providing clarity on this subject is a good reason for studying transport projects, but there are other lessons to be learned.

The Air Transport Action Group (2020) reported that nearly $51.5 billion was spent on airport construction projects in 2018. But, according to ICAO (2020), there are 4,300 airports around the globe that serve scheduled airline service, and two out of every three of these operate at a net loss. This suggests the need with airports to be aware of common factors that lead to poor investment decisions.

Flyvbjerg (2009) explained how the most visible cases of failed infrastructure projects come about in a process that favours "survival of the unfittest" and, in doing so, he drew attention to systematic weaknesses in forecasting, project evaluation and governance arrangements with large projects. These weaknesses will be illustrated in this chapter with airport cases.

As noted, one of the key themes is the role of airports in promoting development. The complexities of planning airports also will be examined, and particular attention will be paid to the risk of obsolescence. Governance is of critical importance because it empowers and incentivises the various actors who contribute to good or bad decisions. A study of failed airport projects illustrates how better decisions can be made - the cases discussed here are too important to dismiss as aberrations in a sector that, too often, delivers poor returns on its assets.

Mirabel International Airport (Montréal, Canada) – Complex decisions, obsolescence and the birth and demise of a major airport.

Mirabel International Airport is one of the best-known examples of a failed airport and the lessons learned from it remain influential. What makes Mirabel particularly interesting is that it illustrates the complexity in planning a large airport and how this increases the propensity to make mistakes. It also is a warning about how airports die because they are vulnerable to obsolescence.

In the 1960s, Montréal was the third largest city in North America and was regarded as a cultural and business centre. The Government of Québec was buoyed by its success in hosting the 1967 International and Universal Exposition – Expo' 67 – which attracted more than 50 million visitors. The belief was that Montréal was poised to take its place as an elite "global city", and further encouragement came when the city was granted the right to host the Summer Olympics in 1976. A problem was that international visitors had to be channelled through Dorval (now Trudeau) International Airport. Traffic at the airport was doubling every eight years and a study undertaken by the Canadian Government concluded that Dorval would exploit all of its expansion options and would be saturated by 1975. Residents in areas near the airport suffered from exposure to noise and were opposed to further expansion.

The Montréal International Airport Study carried out by the Canadian Department of Transport searched for a suitable site for a new airport. Twenty options were evaluated before concluding in favour of a site located 45 kilometres south-west of Montréal which was served by existing road and rail links to Ottawa and Toronto. One of the considerations was that people employed at Dorval would not have needed to change their place of residence. Québec nationalist sentiments also were at play and the Provincial Government chose a site 60 kilometres north-west of Montréal (Groot, 2021).

Mirabel was planned as the largest airport in the world. Edwards (2014) reported that the original land acquisition cost of C$20 million was way too conservative – that the final cost was 760 percent higher! In total the airport cost close to C$500 million. It was not served by good transport links to the city, and with international flights assigned to Mirabel, airlines and passengers were faced with the logistical difficulties of making transfers from Dorval. Although Mirabel's facilities were superior to those at Dorval, passengers preferred Dorval.

Another critical factor that contributed to Mirabel's fate was that it was becoming obsolescent even as it was being built. Montréal had been serving flights enroute between Europe and North America and many of these needed to refuel before crossing the Atlantic Ocean. Aircraft technology took a leap forward in the 1970s and the increasing range and size of aircraft changed the equation. Stopping in Montréal as a transit point was no longer necessary and added costs and inconvenience. Another factor was that significant changes were occurring in aviation policy and regulation that made it possible for other cities, notably Toronto, to become more significant international gateways (Edwards, 2014). Toronto offered more connections without the inconvenience of transferring between airports on opposite sides of the city. The loss of air traffic to Toronto has been cited as a contributing factor to the stagnation of Montréal's economy.

It also was true that hosting the Summer Olympic Games was not an economic success; accumulated debt was a drag on Québec's economy for decades. Passengers were reluctant to use Mirabel and, in 1997 Aéroports de Montréal transferred all scheduled international flights to Dorval. Despite earlier assessments, Dorval (now Trudeau) International Airport was able to accommodate all traffic and, in 2019, 20.3 million passengers moved through its facilities – a level that was expected to have been reached in 1985.

Widely billed as a "white elephant", Mirabel had been used as a racetrack and as a movie set and the runway was used only for general aviation and cargo. The operator, Aéroports de Montréal, tired of meeting the expense of maintaining an empty terminal and chose to demolish it – work that was completed in August 2016. The comments made about Mirabel by Angela Gittens, then Director-General of the Airports Council International are worthy of note:

> ... it takes a long time and a lot of planning to repurpose an airport, and sometimes, it's simply easier to demolish one entirely. There really is no other use for an airport, besides an airport ... This area really could not accommodate two major airports ... airlines hold most of the power when it comes to picking their flight destinations, so there was little Mirabel could do to keep the flights coming in, once airlines decided they liked Trudeau Airport better. And no matter how modern a facility is, a great airfield doesn't bring in customers – customer demand keeps airports alive. (Elliot, 2014)

The story does not end there. The runway remained open, and the number of aircraft movements trebled between 2008 and 2018, with significant growth in cargo operations, flying training, and private jets. A medical supply plant was built on the airport and aerospace companies added to activity levels. Aéroports de Montréal rebranded the airport as "YMX International Aerocity of Mirabel" in May 2019 and has this to say on its website:

> Evolving at the heart of an innovative ecosystem that brings together the major players of the industry in Mirabel and Greater Montreal, YMX is the partner of choice for all companies around the world that wish to establish their business headquarters and their centres of research and innovation on its territory. With the help of YMX, business takes off at Mirabel International Aerocity! (YMX, 2019)

The Mirabel case illustrates all of the features of major infrastructure projects that fail. The long planning horizon adds to their risky nature, though as Mirabel shows – the risk of obsolescence can arise very quickly if planners do not comprehend the game-changing developments occurring around them. Construction is preceded by many years, perhaps decades, of planning and there is a tendency to become locked into particular concepts and locations at an early stage. Planning major airports involves multiple interest groups with different agendas, adding to the technical complexities. An excess of ambition is an ever-present risk.

Typically, there will be a limited number of sites in or around major cities where an airport can be built – taking account of technical requirements and resolution of issues with surrounding communities. Concerns about noise and congestion, taken to their extreme, result in the BANANA syndrome – "build absolutely nothing anywhere near anything/anybody" (Thompson et al., 2013). The danger then is to give rise to a situation when projects that have sound justification are not built. In the case of Montréal, the eventual outcome was to retain the original site where noise was an issue after spending a great deal on a flawed alternative.

Airports are land hungry. They need room to expand over time, but they also need to manage the use of their given allocation of land, and they accomplish this with their "Master Plans". Typically, a Master Plan will look 20 to 30 years ahead, but the decision to construct calls for a different type of analysis – one that focuses on detailed design, costing, evaluation and financing. However, the context in which such analyses can result in "misinformation about costs, benefits, and risks" (Flyvbjerg, 2009, p. 345.

Saint Helena Island and Mattala Rajapaksa International Airports – when can airports lead economic development?

Saint Helena Island is as remote a location as one can find – it lies more than 2,000 kilometres from the nearest landmass lying half-way across the Atlantic Ocean between Africa and South America. The United Kingdom (UK) Government announced in March 2005 that it would fund the airport and that it would complete the project in 2010. In addition to addressing strategic benefits to the UK, air services were intended to overcome isolation for the island's 6,000 residents who previously faced a five-day sea voyage to reach Cape Town.

All of the companies that tendered for the project withdrew their bids by September 2006 because they could not carry out on-site inspections. A new round of tendering commenced in 2006 and three applicants visited the site. The Prime Minister of the UK, Gordon Brown, insisted on personally reviewing and approving the contract. This was awarded to an Italian company but was suspended in November 2008 during the global financial crisis. Subsequently, the project was awarded to Basil Read (Pty) Ltd of South Africa in a design and construct contract valued at £202 million. The UK Government also committed to pay up to £10 million in shared-risk contingency, and £35.1 million for ten years of operation by South African airport operator, Lanseria. However, the contract was not entered into until November 2011 and construction commenced in February 2015. Building an airport in such a remote location was difficult and the cost blew out to £285.5 million. Further delays and costs were incurred in the aerodrome certification process.

One of the justifications for building the airport was that air services would generate tourism and attract cruise ships. In 2010 it was projected that a regular service using a Boeing 737-800 aircraft would bring six thousand visitors in the year it opened and that this number would grow to 30 thousand a year by 2042. A commercial venture sprang up with the aim of building luxury resorts and an international hotel. Although this venture was short-lived, local businesses invested in accommodation facilities only to have their hopes dashed when a test flight on 18 April 2016 exposed a problem of wind shear. Subsequent flights were restricted to smaller aircraft. By now, Basil Read was in financial difficulty and it became necessary for the Saint Helena Government to assume ownership of the airport company, and a weekly air service operated under subsidy. The British press then awarded Saint Helena the title of home to the "world's most useless airport".

Sri Lanka has an airport that, in its current state, is home to real wild elephants (Ratnasabapathy, 2018). Mattala Rajapaksa International Airport (MRIA) was built to address Sri Lanka's need to open a second gateway to the nation. Built adjacent to town where the then President resided, the project was envisaged as a component of a much broader and ambitious plan to transform the town of Hambantota into Sri Lanka's second most important city. A deep-sea port costing US$1.4 billion was another key piece of infrastructure and the vision was for the city to have a large industrial zone, a massive conference centre, a world-class cricket stadium, with housing developments to match. Additionally, it was argued that investments in hotels and resorts would follow based on success in attracting international tourists.

Built at a cost of US$209 million, with more than 90% of this amount being funded by loans, the airport was built to handle a million passengers a year with a runway capable of handling the largest commercial aircraft. One explanation about how the project came to be approved was:

> The story as to how this airport rose and fell is a dive into a quagmire of national politics, geopolitical manoeuvring, raw corruption, and the hunger of China to invest in massive

infrastructure projects along what has subsequently been dubbed the 21st Century Maritime Silk Road. (Shepard, 2016)

The reality was that the economic base where the airport was built consisted of little more than a series of fishing villages surrounded by forests. When a new President was elected, he faced an annual interest obligation of US$17 million for the airport (Shepard, 2016). When MRIA was opened in March 2013, Sri Lankan Airlines, the national carrier, was obliged to operate flights, but the new Government relieved it of this responsibility in 2015. The result was that air services ceased, and one of the unused terminals became a warehouse for storing rice. Shepard reported that 300 soldiers and police officers were deployed to keep wild animals from the nearby forests making their home on the airport premises (Shepard, 2016). Indeed, the airport had become an attraction for tourists coming to see any empty airport where wild elephants roam.

A compelling argument used to justify the construction of airports at Saint Helena Island and at Hambantota in Sri Lanka was that they would stimulate economic development, especially by attracting tourists. It is notable that the ATAG (2020) claimed that aviation contributed $3.5 trillion to the global economy in 2019 and that, as a rough rule of thumb, a thousand workers will be needed to serve each million passengers travelling through an airport. ATAG's claims are supported by a considerable body of evidence from independent studies. Fifty-eight percent of all tourists arrive at their destination on an aircraft (ATAG, 2020) and there are many examples where airport improvements and new airline services have put destinations "on the map". However, all of this empirical and real-world evidence does not guarantee success.

The evidence is that the direction of causality between investment in transport infrastructure and development works in both directions, but what matters is the pre-existing state of development. A recent study into how long-haul connections between cities results in growth and trade and flows of investments and expertise reaffirmed this conclusion:

> ... it does not matter if a place got lucky in terms of potential connections, if very few would want to fly there anyway. This means that poor places also miss out on the convergence potential induced by increased business links and the capital flows embedded in them. This suggests that while long-range connections can foster development, one has to be in a position to catch that figurative plane. In its aerial dimension, at least, globalization can help some places take off, but others seem to get left behind on the runway. (Campante & Yanagizawa-Drott, 2018)

This fact has been understood for many decades, but it has to be repeated given the tendency to justify "transformational" projects based on extrapolations of a broadly valid argument. Necessary conditions for economic development to occur include: the capability to benefit from improved connectivity (e.g. a suitably qualified labour force and a dynamic economy); a receptive environment for investment; and a complementary policy and legal framework with supporting government commitments.

It is true that sustainable development goals encompass objectives other than economic development, but the point considered here is how much weight can be placed on the argument that airports should be developed to lead economic growth, especially through tourism. Saint Helena Island and Hambantota, Sri Lanka illustrate cases where underlying conditions required for development were absent.

Wasteful spending thrives in forests of weak governance

The European Regional Development Fund and the European Union's (EU) Cohesion Fund provided funds for airport developments that, according to the European Court of Auditors (ECA) were wasted because they were "too close to each other and do not contribute to regional accessibility or development" (European Court of Auditors, 2014). The Auditors concluded that, between 2000 and 2013, the EU's commitment of €666 million for airport infrastructure at 20 airports in Estonia, Greece, Italy, Poland and Spain provided little value for money.

One of the factors contributing to waste was that, once funds were committed to national bodies, there was a reluctance to reallocate the money away from airports even when the justification for the projects was weak. Most of these airports, encountered delays of two years in construction, and more than half went over budget so that the member states had to top up funding by another €100 million. More than half of the airports failed to realise projected traffic numbers, and one case, Cordoba, had fewer than 7,000 passengers in 2013, considerably fewer than the prediction of 179,000. Most of the airports had less than 100,000 passengers a year and required ongoing funding to support operation and maintenance.

The case of Spain's Ciudad Real Central International Airport (CRCIA) is a stark example of the waste that arises when incentives favour construction over ongoing viability. The airport was envisaged as an alternative to Madrid's Barajas airport and cost its private owners more than €1 billion. The prevailing situation in Spain was that finance was readily available from local banks amidst a nation-wide construction boom. A senior journalist, Miguel Angel Bastenier, commented that "There was such a frenzy for investing money and people got inebriated" (Harter, 2012).

Local politicians were represented on the board of the bank, and the promoter happened to be a construction magnate whose plan enjoyed bipartisan political support. Loans were taken out purely to cover the construction and little thought seems to have been given to what it would cost to operate. There were claims as well that the promoters benefited from construction contracts. It appears that there was an assumption that the regional government would subsidise airlines to fly to CRCIA and that accountability in the public sector was weak (Harter, 2012).

When CRCIA finally opened, Spain was in the grips of a severe financial crisis. Caja Castilla-La Mancha, the regional bank that was Ciudad's main shareholder, became the first of the Spanish banks to be bailed out by the national government. Of course, the projected passenger numbers never materialised, and the airport was forced to close. It joined other defunct airports in becoming a place for testing fast cars and for making films. When the receivers put the airport up for auction in July 2015, they set a reserve price of €28,000, but the highest bidder was €10,000 - 100,000 times less than it cost to build (Fenton, 2015).

These cases illustrate how poorly conceived projects proliferate when there is weak governance, and the private sector can be a willing accomplice in wasteful spending. There are more than 650 airports, out of the world's 4,300 airports serving scheduled flights, that have some degree of private sector participation (ICAO, 2020, p.78). Yet they handle more than 40 percent of global traffic and, mostly, the evidence is that they are financially sound and are well managed.

But the fact is that two out of every three airports operate at a net loss. Most of them handle fewer than one million passengers a year, and the "net profits of a minority of high-traffic airports significantly exceed the net losses of the majority of smaller airports" (ICAO, 2020, p.78). Airports handling fewer than 200,000 passengers per annum are likely to incur annual losses.

Planning for airports generally begins with forecasts of

movements of passengers, cargo and aircraft. However, forecasters do not have crystal balls when they make their projections for several decades. Forecasting errors arise when the data on which they are based is flawed, or when inappropriate analytical methods are applied. One way to deliver more credible forecasts is to have them prepared by a competent and independent entity, though even this can be problematic. There are ways to improve forecasting and to allow flexibility in designing facilities, but good governance certainly requires a culture that discourages deliberate misrepresentation.

Similarly, a supporting culture is critical when carrying out cost-benefit analyses (CBA), feasibility studies and business plans. Flyvbjerg expressed pessimism on this score and warned that "cost–benefit analysis … is not to be trusted for major infrastructure projects" (ICAO, 2020, p.78). Thompson et al. (2013) were more positive about the capability of CBA to take a "wide ranging consideration of both the positive and negative impacts of airport expansion" (ICAO, 2020, p.78). They had in mind that the framework of CBA can encompass economic impact studies.

The incentives to misrepresent benefits and costs and to dress up justification for a project in deceptive, but convincing technical reports can be addressed through measures designed to improve accountability and transparency and by addressing power relationships. Putting these matters to one side, even well-intentioned analysts can reach erroneous conclusions. A natural tendency to underestimate costs and overestimate benefits can be the most problematic root cause of faulty evaluations. Behavioural economists understand that there can be a tendency for analysts to overemphasise recent events. Planners in Montréal could have been guilty of "optimism \ bias" because they would have been familiar with past successes, and this could have resulted in an underestimate of unfavourable outcomes. Planners are less likely to place weight on matters that are outside their range of expertise or experience and that might explain why the "environmental" factors that rendered Mirabel obsolete were not recognised.

Flyvbjerg argued that large, complex projects with long lives are inherently risky and that a better way to proceed is with "reference class forecasting". Essentially, what he was referring to is what model developers call "external validity" (ICAO, 2020, p.78). Internal validity is ensured by applying models in ways that are consistent with underlying theory and technical requirements. External validity requires the analyst to stand back and consider whether the results stack up against observed conditions. What it would require is for airport analysts to have a sound knowledge about the experiences of a reference set of comparable airports. Certainly, failed airports need to be included in this reference set.

The Mirabel case illustrates the fact that airport infrastructure projects all face significant risks of obsolescence. Arguably, major airports have become victims of their own success. Terminals have become larger, and the biggest airports have multiple terminals. But these sprawling facilities are costly to operate and present challenges to passengers who are transferring between flights. After the terrorist acts perpetrated on aviation in the USA on 11 September 2001, added security standards and procedures were introduced. All of this consumed additional space. Now the world is experiencing a global health emergency with the Covid-19 virus. All airports will find it difficult to accommodate recommendations for social distancing and additional screening and processing.

Is it possible to eliminate failures with airport projects?

Failed airport projects are extreme and obvious cases of poor investment decisions, and, if history is the judge, mistakes will continue to be made in the future. Indeed, the uncertainties introduced by Covid-19 and growing concerns about how air travel contributes to climate change could lead to an increase in obsolescent airports. A question that needs to be posed is whether the planners, because of their cognitive limitations, are failing to give sufficient weight to unfamiliar, but game-changing events unfolding in their commercial and operating environment?

One path to getting better value for money is to focus on governance − to ensure that incentives and soft budget constraints do not work in perverse ways. Better governance requires accountability and transparency. Thus, a second question that should be posed is whether the validity of forecasts and project appraisals has been assessed by independent experts? However, it should be borne in mind that even a satisfactory answer to this test is no guarantee of success.

Considering that many airports do not earn a respectable rate of return on their assets, and that the majority of small airports struggle to break-even, the need for financial discipline is clear. Even well-intentioned analysts are prone to biased judgements, whether they are conscious of it or not, and it helps if additional perspectives are brought to bear, including examination of comparable projects. Techniques matter, but the hallmarks of a good evaluation culture are when all team members seek credible answers to basic questions including: what is the objective of the project; how will it be done; is this the best way; is this the best time to do it; what is required in support to make the project a success/avoid its failure; and what is the operational and maintenance plan?

Airport projects are highly visible and often are supported by arguments about the wider economic and social benefits expected to flow from them. The claim can be credible, but as this chapter has pointed out – conducive conditions need to exist. Thus, it is critically important to ask questions along the lines "what underlying conditions are required before wider benefits will materialise, and are they satisfied?"

Airport white elephants are cases we should not forget. Understanding how they came about is relevant both to decisions about new projects as well as to providing lessons for other airports to avoid having facilities that become obsolescent in a rapidly changing world.

References

Air Transport Action Group (2020, September 30). Aviation: Benefits beyond borders. https://aviationbenefits.org/downloads/aviation-benefits-beyond-borders-2020/

Campante, F., & Yanagizawa-Drott, D. (2018). Long-range growth: economic development in the global network of air links. *The Quarterly Journal of Economics*, *133*(3), 1395-1458. https://doi.org/10.1093/qje/qjx050

Edwards, B. (2014, January 24). Canada's messy history of big ticket airport projects, from Mirabel to Porter and Pickering. *The Toronto Review of Books*.. https://torontoreviewofbooks.com/2014/01/canadas-messy-history-big-ticket-airport-projects-mirabel-porter-pickering/

Elliott, J. (2014, August 20). Montreal's abandoned Mirabel Airport too costly to repurpose. *CTVNews.ca*. https://www.ctvnews.ca/canada/montreal-s-abandoned-mirabel-airport-too-costly-to-repurpose-1.1967712

European Court of Auditors (2014). *EU-funded airport infrastructures: poor value for money. Special Report No. 21*. E.C.A., Luxembourg.

https://www.eca.europa.eu/Lists/ECADocuments/SR14_21/QJAB14021ENC.pdf

Fenton, S. (2015, July 19). Spanish 'ghost airport' that cost €1bn to build sells at auction for €10,000. *The Independent*. https://www.independent.co.uk/news/world/europe/spanish-ghost-airport-cost-eu1bn-build-sells-auction-eu10-000-10399433.html

Flyvbjerg, B. (2009). Survival of the unfittest: Why the worst infrastructure gets built – and what we can do about it. *Oxford Review of Economic Policy*, *25*(3), 344-67. https://doi.org/10.1093/oxrep/grp024

Groot, M. (2021, January 30). Montréal-Mirabel International Airport. Part 1: A grand vision. *Airport.History.org*. https://www.airporthistory.org/mirabel-1.html.

Harter, P. (2012, July 26). The white elephants that dragged Spain into the red. *BBC News, Spain*. https://www.bbc.com/news/magazine-18855961

International Civil Aviation Organization (2020). Performance in numbers: world airport data. In *International Civil Aviation Organization, World of civil aviation report*. 4, 65-80. ICAO. https://store.icao.int/en/icao-world-civil-aviation-report-wcar

Ratnasabapathy, R. (2018, March 9). The white-elephant airport with real elephants. *Adam Smith Institute*. https://www.adamsmith.org/blog/white-elephants#:~:text=The%20white-elephant%20airport%20%28which%20serves%20no%20airlines%29%20has%2C,animals%29%2C%20since%20it%20sits%20by%20a%20wildlife%20sanctuary

Shepard, D. (2016, May 28). The story behind the world's emptiest international airport. Forbes. https://www.forbes.com/sites/wadeshepard/2016/05/28/the-story-behind-the-worlds-emptiest-international-airport-sri-lankas-mattala-rajapaksa/?sh=2a9040717cea

Thompson, D., Perkins, S. & and Van Dender, K. (2013, December). Expanding airport capacity under constraints in large urban areas. Discussion Paper No 2013-24, Joint *OECD/ITF Transport Research*

Centre, International Transport Forum, Paris, France. http://hdl.handle.net/10419/97086

YMX (2021). *International Aerocity of Mirabel* (Webpage). https://www.admtl.com/en/business

CASE STUDY 9

White Elephants of the Sea: Australia's Disastrous Future Submarine Program

Binoy Kampmark

It was born in the insecure minds of establishment megalomania. Australia's desperate effort to add to a naval arms race in the Asia-Pacific region, termed the SEA 1000 Future Submarine Program, has become the notable white elephant in the annals of defence and planning. From the start, the choice for the proposed French-made diesel-powered submarines based on a nuclear-powered model seemed audaciously peculiar. Australia had avoided purchasing more appropriate, medium-sized submarines from a conventional submarine maker, opting, instead, for a nuclear submarine design that would be retooled for conventional use. This was ironic for a country that is the world's third largest exporter of uranium.

The irony, it should be said, did not stop there. In September 2021, with the announcement of the AUKUS security relationship comprising Australia, the United Kingdom and the United States, the status of the Barracuda as a premier white elephant of the sea was assured. The three-way security agreement promising greater "integrated defence" and a more robust "defence posture" gave Canberra an undertaking that submarines with nuclear propulsion would, in decades, be assured. With no actual design plan in place for these new submarines, one white elephant of the sea risks being replaced by another.

Background

One only gets into the submarine procurement business to spite government treasurers and minders of the public purse. Efficiency and effectuality are incidental matters. Submarines of stealth may turn out to be detectable in their clumsiness. The costs they incur through maintenance can prove astronomical. The disaster that is Australia's SEA 1000 Future Submarine program is a superb case in point, a white elephant of the sea that began as a contract between Canberra and France's DCNS, now Naval Group, in 2016.

Australia's Future Submarine Program (FSP) known as Project SEA 1000 (Brangwin, 2020) had its gestation in the 2009 Defence White Paper (Aust. Govt., 2009, May 4) and the Defence Capability Plan 2009 (Aust. Govt., 2009, July 6). Three contenders duly emerged: France, Germany and Japan. In the background was always a nagging doubt: were these submarines even necessary?

In 2014, it seemed that the Japanese naval industry had what the Abbott government wanted: the means to build 12 submarines. The Royal Australian Navy (RAN), however, disliked what was offer. The Japanese group failed to confirm that it would boost local skilled jobs in Australia, even as it was being outmanoeuvred by German and French contenders. The French contenders, in particular, smelled a catch, employing Sean Costello, the CEO of the Australian branch of the French defence contractor DCNS, to tempt officials in Canberra.

In November 2014, DCNS CEO Hervé Guillou convinced French Defence Minister Jean-Yves Le Drian to visit Australia.

In Albany, French and Australian officials congregated to commemorate the first sailing of Australian soldiers to France in the First World War. With Prime Minister Tony Abbott being deposed in a palace coup by his Liberal rival Malcolm Turnbull, attention turned towards the French alternative. In 2016, a AU$50 billion contract duly followed, promising 12 French-designed submarines from the originally named DCNS (of which 62 per cent is owned by the French government) supplied to the RAN. (This cost, as discussed later, would be revised.) Guillou initially praised the "strong teamwork between the French authorities, DCNS and our industrial partners" speaking of a Franco-Australian alliance more than a century old (Tomkins, 2016).

The French had good reason to cheer. For one, Australian decision makers had seemingly forgotten previous purchases of French military hardware that had caused technical problems or were of limited utility (Cowan, 2021). In Paris, there was much gloating amongst those in the military establishment at having secured the, as L'Express (2016) termed it, "contract of the century". Resident naval astrologers looked at the stars and suggested 4000 jobs would be created in France alone. French Defence Minister Jean-Yves Le Drian proclaimed that a "50-year marriage" had been entered into (Tertrais, 2021). Dirigisme has worked again. The returns for Australia, for seeking out a contract of minimal worth in security at considerable cost to the budget, promised to be leaner.

Attack Class Submarines: intentions, assessments, delusions

The broader context for selecting the French project lay in a long obsession of the Australian defence establishment with submarines. The SEA 1000 Future Submarine program was a project intended to provide a submarine capability that would eventually replace the long standing, problematic Collins Class. The Collins class itself was called Australia's "Holden amongst submarines," a comparison that should have furnished sufficient warning of what was to come. In Dobell's apt observation, "Subs are a fundamental element of the bipartisan consensus on defence. But the love quickly becomes agony and angst when we turn to building them" (Dobell, 2020).

The incentive for acquiring more submarines was a motivation as old as it was unoriginal: everyone else was doing it. With the region engaged in an underwater arms-race, Australia risked missing out. As the 2016 Defence White Paper explained, replacing the six CCSMs with 12 future submarines was necessary given that half of the world's submarines would be operating in the Indo-Pacific region by 2035 (Australian Government, 2016, p. 90).

When the intergovernmental agreement to construct twelve Shortfin Barracuda Block 1A submarines was signed in 2016, the French military establishment could triumphantly claim that they had won a coup over rival arms manufacturers. As an Australian government announcement went in April 2016, "The decision was driven by DCNS's ability to best meet all of the Australian Government requirements. These included superior sensor performance and stealth characteristics, as well as range and endurance similar to the Collins class submarine. The Government's considerations also included cost, schedule, program execution, through-life support and Australian industry involvement" (Tomkins, 2016). *Defence Connect* (2019, July 19) also noted such lofty expectations, with the Attack Class submarine "expected to deliver a quantum leap in the capability delivered to the Royal Australian Navy and its submarine service by leveraging technology and capabilities developed for nuclear submarines, implemented on a conventional submarine". Be wary of leaping submarines with leveraged technology.

Initially, the cost of the project was projected at AU$50 billion. But by May 2018, it became clear that the picture was somewhat dearer. Rear Admiral Greg Sammut had to concede to Australian senators in a Senate estimates hearing that another AU$50 billion would be required to sustain the submarines for the duration of their operating life. In explaining this to Senator Rex Patrick of the Centre Alliance, Sammut heeded lessons from the civil service school of obfuscation. "Many of the detailed costs of acquisition and sustainment will be determined during the design process through choices made but at this point early estimation of the sustainment costs for the fleet are of the order of up to $50 billion on a constant price basis".

The implications in such an observation were ominous to those in Treasury. The expenditure for the submarine program would only rise, with the cost of sustaining these naval creations being anywhere from two to three times that of their acquisition price. "It's disturbing that Defence has done this", remarked Senator Patrick at the time.

In any other context, this would be regarded as gross negligence, but defence costs operate in another realm of insensible and tolerated practice. And just to illustrate the point, over the course of five months in 2020, the submarine project cost Australian taxpayers a further AU$10 billion, occasioned by currency fluctuations and an oversight on the planned commencement date for the construction of HMAS *Attack*, intended as the fleet's lead boat.

The rising cost of the program also caught the attention of other politicians as well. One Nation's Senator Malcolm Roberts, while idiosyncratic on such matters as climate science, was firmly grounded in questioning the level of expenditure. In May 2020, he, in his own words, "took time to condemn the new contract signed to build 12 new submarines." To his fellow senators, he asked whether the government had taken leave of its senses during times of the COVID-19 pandemic. "In the middle of this pandemic we cannot afford to proceed with this contract. This money will be far better spent to support the Australian recovery from the economic pit, that is caused by this pandemic. By the time these submarines are delivered, they will be obsolete".

This was not an ill-informed view. Within Canberra's strategic community there were also concerns that the Attack program was being readied for obsolescence even before it had gotten off the design board. "One of the questions Defence Minister Linda Reynolds should ask about the Attack-class program is how to avoid spending $4 billion apiece on a 21st century maritime equivalent of the Gladiator". The Gladiator, remark Woolner and Glynne-Jones (2019), was a biplane which entered service with the Royal Air Force in February 1937, by which time it was already obsolete before the arrival of the Hawker Hurricane later that year. While the goal of Defence was to produce, in its own lofty terms, a "regionally superior" submarine, various countries in the region were already putting that aim in jeopardy. Japan, for instance, had launched a submarine with a lithium-ion main battery design; South Korea had approved the construction of similar battery-powered submarines and Naval Group itself was developing its own version for use in its *Scorpene* class (Woolner & Glynne-Jones, 2019.

Deviations, disparities and concerns

It did not take long for critics to note divergences from the intended plan and its gradual unfolding. In January 2020, the Australian National Audit Office weighed in with a report outlining the risks in the SEA 1000 program, even at its incipient stages. "The decision not to acquire a military-off-the-shelf submarine platform, and instead engage a 'strategic partner' to design and deliver the submarines with significant Australian industry input, has increased the risk of this acquisition". Delays were already taking place in the design phase; "contracted milestones" had been extended. The ANAO also had a nugget of enlightenment: the government's own Naval Shipbuilding Advisory Board, comprising US admirals previously receptive to the French proposal, suggested that Australia walk away from its contract with Naval Group.

The following month, such concerns worried the Department of Defence and Naval Group with sufficient urgency to warrant a firm rebuke to naysayers in a joint statement. "Sovereign control over the Attack Class submarine fleet and maximising Australian industry involvement throughout all phases of the Attack Class Submarine program are contracted objectives in the strategic partnering agreement between Defence and Naval Group". Australian industry would also be "systematically" approached "to identify suitable suppliers of the vast array of equipment to be fitted to the submarine, ranging from hydraulic systems to galley equipment".

Minister for Defence Linda Reynolds was unimpressed with Naval Group Australia CEO John Davis, who had expressed his frank concerns about the project to journalists, generally approving of the findings of the ANAO report. "I am disappointed by comments attributed to Naval Group Australia as they do not reflect the strong collaboration between Naval Group and Australian industry on this program of national significance" (*Australian Defence Magazine*, 2020).

The Minister's disappointment would not have been helped by a damning report commissioned by Submarines for Australia, conducted by Insight Economics and released in March 2020. It noted how the Naval Group was pushing back on incorporating "Australian content"; the presence of a "dangerous capability gap" given delays in the project; and the "questionable strategic value" of the entire effort. Gary Johnston of Submarines for Australia was crushing in his critique: the Australian-French contract was based on "dumbing down a nuclear submarine by removing the whole basis of its superior capability, and then charging at least twice as much for a far less capable submarine" (Johnson, 2020). The French contractor had been selected even prior to the finalisation of any preliminary design, before the project could be seriously assessed in terms of costs, and in the absence of a tough negotiating stance from the diplomats in Canberra.

The report further suggested revisiting the Collins submarine to develop a more advanced version which would constitute the necessary competition for the Attack class. The parties behind the winning design would then reach a fixed price contract to deliver the submarines. "On the basis of expert professional advice, we consider that an evolved Collins 2.0 submarine, with a comparable ability to Attack, could be delivered at least five years earlier, at a much lower cost and with 70 per cent of local content."

Veteran strategist Hugh White, in launching the Insight Economics report at the National Press Club, was also of the view the project needed to be reconsidered. "This is the biggest conventional submarine in the world by far and will be very complex to design and build." Even if it did stick to schedule, it would only be in service in the mid-2030s. He was impressed by the idea that competition for the Attack class design would be developed at the modest cost of $100 million "and without delaying delivery" (White, 2020).

In addition to this, rumours also began circulating that the Morrison government was considering the possibility of acquiring the Type 214 diesel electric submarine developed by Howaldstwerker-Deutsche Werft GmbH (HDW) to fill the "capability gap" as the government awaited the delivery of the

Attack Class complement.

The problems between Naval Group and Canberra were unsettling enough to lead the RAN to commence an internal inquiry examining a range of options. The lead on the inquiry, Vice Admiral Jonathan Mead, had warned the Morrison government that the Attack-class would fail to enter service in a timely way relative to the worsening strategic circumstances facing Australia (Packham, 2021). Taking the view of Submarines for Australia, one suggestion involved bringing in the original designer of the Collins class submarine, Saab Kockums, to work alongside the Australian owned entity ASC Pty Ltd (formerly Australian Submarine Corporation) as part of a project extending the lives of the existing six submarines. Yet another option involved Saab pursuing a $50 million-$100 million scoping study of a "Son of Collins" design, which would work off a Dutch navy long-range version (Tillett, 2021).

Questions about the amount of Australian industry content continued to plague the contract well into 2021. Suspicions remained that the agreement was, at heart, a French driven enterprise, with a duped Australia limping along with the cash. According to the *Australian Financial Review* (2021, June 18), Canberra continued to show growing disgruntlement over the division of work between French labour and Australian contractors. The latter were meant to be doing 60% of the share, though the arrangement was never settled. In May 2021, the dispute between the Defence Department and Naval Group had reached a point of such acrimony as to lead to a freeze by the French concern on hiring more staff in France and a halt in spending money on aspects of the project in the absence of any reimbursement guarantee from Canberra. As Naval Group's Transfer of Technology program manager Fabrice Leduc described it to his staff, the submarine project had been subjected to a "political timeline" following a change of minister in the Defence portfolio. The new occupant, Peter Dutton, was biding his time because "he wanted to have some strong warranties from the industry and especially Naval Group in terms of cost and schedule." This less than flattering assessment was rejected by a spokeswoman for Dutton. But Leduc was convinced that the firm needed to be financially prudent in future dealings with Canberra. "My strategy will be to engage in topics in which we are 100 per cent sure we will be reimbursed by the Commonwealth" (Tillett, 2021).

Dissolving the marriage

On September 15, 2021 a stunning announcement was made by the leaders of Australia, the United Kingdom and the United States. The secretly negotiated trilateral security pact AUKUS effectively sank the Naval Group contract with a commitment "to a shared ambition to support Australia in acquiring nuclear-powered submarines for the Royal Australian Navy". Expertise from both the UK and the US would be drawn on to "bring an Australian capability into service at the earliest achievable date" (Biden, Johnson & Morrison, 2021). The agreement had been made without consulting France, enraging President Emmanuel Macron.

No contracts, as yet, have been drawn out. The costs continue to remain the stuff of speculative fantasy. We are not sure about whether the nuclear-powered alternative with Anglo-American blessing will be based on the US Virginia class or UK Astute class. In many ways, the state of affairs for Australia, from a sovereign, naval perspective is worse than what it was with the Naval Group agreement: no contract, no design, and a hazy date for service sometime in the 2040s.

Australia also lacks a shipyard able to build or maintain such vessels, an infrastructural defect ignored by Prime Minister

Scott Morrison's praise of South Australia as "home to some of the most skilled shipbuilding workers in the world" replete with "know-how, ingenuity, industrial knowledge and determination". The only concrete detail we are left with is a promise from Morrison to engage in an 18-month "intense examination of what we need to do to exercise our nuclear stewardship responsibilities here in Australia" (Aust. Govt., 2021).

The troubling picture emerging here is that this next, nuclear powered white elephant promises to be part of a greater militarisation of Australia with a cast iron commitment to any conflict waged by the US in the Indo-Pacific. AUKUS entraps Australia within tighter security arrangements, utilising its resources and bases for a broader projection of US power in the Indo-Pacific. This point was made by a retired US submarine admiral to *USNI News* (2021, Sep 15). "Maintenance was a big factor in limiting [our deployments]". The agreement, former US National Security Council member Barry Pavel similarly confirmed, would also enable "US submarine access to Australian support infrastructure" as part of Washington's "increasingly 'latticed' defence posture" (*New Atlanticist*, 2021, Sept. 15).

Australia's Defence Minister Peter Dutton, speaking in Washington, painted a picture of a future garrison state, with Australia becoming the base for "rotational deployments of all types of US military aircraft". He envisaged an increase in the number of US Marines to add to the current complement of 5,000 on rotation in the Northern Territory, including more bases and 'the storage of different ordnances'. US Navy commanders are already getting giddy at the prospect of using Australia as a location for maintaining US attack vessels.

The fare arising from the dissolution of the union with Naval Group was ultimately settled by the succeeding Albanese Labor government. The divorce tag came in at $835 million.

"This is a saving from the $5.5 billion that Senate estimates was told would result from that program," stated Australia's new Prime Minister Anthony Albanese. "But it still represents an extraordinary waste from a government that was always big on announcement but not good on delivery, and from a government that will be remembered as the most wasteful government in Australia's history since federation" (Doran, 2022). To this can be added the $3.4 billion already spent.

Enduring lessons

The first salient lesson in the exercise of submarine acquisitions is cost. It is accepted globally that building and then operating submarines is a taxing exercise on a country's treasury. Submarine projects have a habit of bungling in execution and costly in consequence. From the outset, the costing for the SEA 1000 project proved problematic. By late 2015, prior to the Defence Department receiving industry responses through its "competitive evaluation tender", a tag of $50 billion was decided upon. By the time a defence white paper was released on February 25 the following year dealing with the integrated investment program, the industry responses had been received. The only change to this total, at this point, was a tentative addition of a "greater than" sign to the figure: >$50bn (Hellyer, 2020). "Defence works in out-turned dollars, which takes inflation into account, and there was nothing in the 2016 investment program to suggest the number was different" (Hellyer, 2020). But as already noted, Rear Admiral Greg Sammut, in a Senate estimates hearing in late May 2018, painted a different picture, suggesting that the $50 billion figure was based "on a constant price basis". The Parliamentary Library Research Service went further in noting that operating and maintaining the submarines until 2080 would cost an additional $50 billion, not inclusive of inflation, with a total of $145 billion (Brangwin, 2020).

What had happened was an increase in costs even as the competitive evaluation process was underway. Hellyer suggests one of two reasons. The first: that the initial outturned figure of $50 billion was, by that early stage, already too low. The Australian Strategic Policy Institute's own 2008 estimate for a $36.5 billion constant, when rebaselined to 2015, reaches a figure of $42 billion. When outturned, it balloons to $67 billion. The second reason: the need for more exacting performance requirements. The 2016 white paper took the edge of the future submarine's strategic role. The cost assessment following that would have been lower. And yet, the same document is grandiose in asserting that the existing fleet of six Collins Class submarines will be replaced by "12 regionally superior submarines". As Hellyer (2020) puts it, "If anything was going to lead to an open-ended expansion of requirements, that would be it".

Pick the right submarine

This is always contentious, given disagreements about Australia's actual defence needs. In the context of the Attack class, the submarine's ushering into service should have tallied with the shelf-life of the Collins Class to prevent any perceived capability gap. The fact that it did not was largely based on assumptions that the life of the Collins Class could be extended. But even then, the gap between the signing of the contract and the arrival of the first Attack class vessels threatened the vessels with obsolescence.

Andrew Davies, another senior fellow of ASPI, makes a range of salient observations about the nature of modern conventional submarines. For one, they come a poor second in terms of performance to nuclear submarines when it comes to hunting today's more formidable ships in terms of speed and submerged endurance. The current operating doctrine for conventional submarines rested upon waiting for transiting targets to reach the submarine, which would lay waiting at maritime "choke points". He suggests that the trends are towards a more sophisticated role of IRS (intelligence, surveillance and reconnaissance), which would make the life of such submarines potentially short-lived and far from covert. "We are investing many billions of dollars to get small, incremental improvements in stealth, range and endurance while the counter-technologies are on the cusp of massive, and potentially relatively cheap, increases in performance" (Davies, 2019).

The corollary of selecting the submarine is whether an existing, off-the-shelf model is purchased, or whether it requires domestic design construction. Dobell appropriately calls this the clash of two world views: that of Customer Oz and Industry Oz. Such different approaches were starkly illustrated, and subsequently politicised, by Abbott's preference for a ready-made Japanese model, and Turnbull's preference for one that would be constructed in Australia.

The AUKUS component pushing Australia towards submarines with nuclear propulsion does little to resolve this dilemma, with Canberra lacking the expertise in virtually every aspect of the field. The enterprise will essentially be a primarily US-UK driven one, with minimal Australian involvement. The date by which such vessels are promised leaves the defence establishment with few options other than to refurbish a more modern version of the Collin Class. And by the time the nuclear submarines do make a showing, the environment, as Paul Keating observes with acid accuracy in his National Press Club address (2021, November 9), would have already changed.

Staffing and division of labour

The issue of not having firm and clear commitments on staffing divisions and industrial content was a crucial issue in the contract with Naval. The estimate of having 60 per cent of content coming from Australian sources was never put on solid footing. This gave the French contractor ample leeway to dictate terms. An additional and important factor was that, even if the twelve Attack Class vessels had ever found their way into the Royal Australian Navy, staffing would have remained an issue. This problem continues to afflict the existing Collins submarines, which have also provided a fair share of problems during their time in service. Marcus Hellyer of the Australian Strategic Policy Institute sees the effort to find adequate numbers of submariners as a vital feature of the transition process (Hellyer, 2018). With AUKUS it is also unclear, given the training and structural requirements that will be needed for nuclear-propelled submarines, how this problem will be resolved. While the US and UK have committed to a sharing relationship on such technology, the terms remain vague and will constitute part of the 18-month scoping agreement.

Conclusions

The SEA 1000 effort has proven to be a striking example of Maginot Line thinking: we need this to make a statement, because other countries happen to be playing in the same waters. The tendency towards error and bungling, notably when it comes to acquiring and maintaining a submarine arm in defence, are consistent. Defence procurement, especially in the field of submarine acquisition, shows itself to be a game for dunces.

Ominously for Australia's defence, the country now risks repeating the mistakes of the Naval Group contract with variations. No contract of supply for the nuclear-powered submarines has been drawn up with the US and UK. The horizon as to when these submarines will become operational is even farther than that of the Attack class, with assessments predicting 2040 as the first year of delivery. Dutton has tried to soften the revelation by claiming he was interested, when defence minister, in purchasing two Virginia-class submarines from the US by 2030 (Karp, 2022). Australian naval personnel, as things stand, have no expertise in the field of managing nuclear submarines and will require training. The country lacks a shipyard for constructing such vessels, meaning that any initial work and skills will effectively be outsourced to Anglo-American personnel. As Sam Roggeveen of the Lowy Institute reminds us, the 18-month consultation process announced by Morrison will not focus on the merits of the program but how it will be implemented (*The Interpreter*, September 16, 2021).

And, just to make matters worse, Australia has done its best in souring its strategic relationship with a regional power in the Indo-Pacific. In this dance of naval white elephants, Canberra has been accused by no less a person than President Macron himself, of mendacity, bad faith and insensitivity. The costs on that front promise to be significant, even as the future of the next white elephant of the sea is determined.

References

Australian Defence Magazine (2020, February 14). https://www.australiandefence.com.au/adm/digital-editions

Australian Government (2009, May 4). *Defending Australia in the Asia Pacific century: Force 2030.* Department of Defence. 70-71 https://www.defence.gov.au/sites/default/files/2021 08/defence_white_paper_2009.pdf

Australian Government (2009, July 6). *Defence capability plan 2009.*

Department of Defence. 171-172. https://defence.gov.au/publications/docs/DCP_2009.pdf

Australian Government (2016, February 25). *2016 Defence white paper.* Department of Defence.

https://www.defence.gov.au/sites/default/files/2021-08/2016-Defence-White-Paper.pdf

Australian Government (2021, September 16). Key naval projects confirmed for South Australia. Joint media release (Scott Morrison & Simon Birmingham). Department of Defence. https://www.minister.defence.gov.au/minister/peter-dutton/media-releases/key-naval-projects-confirmed-south-australia.

Biden, J., Johnson, B. and Morrison, S. (2021, September 15). Joint Leaders Statement on AUKUS. Statements and Releases. The White House. https://www.whitehouse.gov/briefing-room/statements-releases/2021/09/15/joint-leaders-statement-on-aukus/

Brangwin, N. (2020, February 26). *Managing SEA 1000: Australia's attack class submarines* (Research Paper Series 2019-29). Parliament Library (Commonwealth of Australia). https://parlinfo.aph.gov.au/parlInfo/download/library/prspub/7206909/upload_binary/7206909.pdf

Cowan, C. (2021, May 3). The 'Contract of the Century: France reacts to the Australian submarine deal. *The Strategist.* https://www.aspistrategist.org.au/the-contract-of-the-century-france-reacts-to-the-australian-submarine-deal/

Davies, A. (2020, October 22). Australia should bring forward planned submarine technology review. *The Strategist.* https://www.aspistrategist.org.au/australia-should-bring-forward-planned-submarine-technology-review/.

Dobell, G. (2020, August 17). The strange submarine saga: vital yet vexed. *The Strategist.* https://www.aspistrategist.org.au/the-strange-submarine-saga-vital-yet-vexed/#:~:text=For%20a%20couple%20of%20decades,the%20political%20and%20defence%20classes

Doran, M. (2022, June 11). Australian government agrees to pay $835 million to French submarine contractor Naval Group over cancelled contract. ABC News. https://www.abc.net.au/news/2022-06-11/albanese-submarine-deal-with-france/101145042.

Hellyer, M. (2018, October 18). Thinking through submarine transition. *Australian Strategic Policy Institute.* https://www.aspi.org.au/report/thinking-through-submarine-transition

Hellyer, M. (2020, April 28). Has the cost of Australia's future submarines gone up? Part 2. *The Strategist.* https://www.aspistrategist.org.au/has-the-cost-of-australias-future-submarines-gone-up-part-2/

Johnson, G. (2020, March 11). *Submarines for Australia, Australia's Future Submarine: Do We Need a Plan B?* Insight Economics. 5-6. https://submarinesforaustralia.com.au/sea/wp-content/uploads/Australias-Future-Submarine-Insight-Economics-report-11-March-2020.pdf

Karp, P. (2022, June 10). Peter Dutton's claim he planned to buy US nuclear subs is 'political point-sscoring', defence experts say. *The Guardian.* https://www.theguardian.com/australia-news/2022/jun/10/peter-duttons-claim-he-planned-to-buy-us-nuclear-subs-political-point-scoring-defence-experts-say.

L'Express. (2016, April 26). Vente de sous-marins à l'Australie des 'milliers d'emplois en France'. http://lexpansion.lexpress.fr/actualite-economique/le-francais-dcns-decroche-un-contrat-a-34-milliards-d-euros-pour-des-sous-marins_1786232.html

Packham, B (2021, May 5). Collins upgrade may plug submarine gap. *The Australian.*

Tertrais, B. (2021, April 28). In French-Australian submarine deal, broader political and strategic context mattered. *The Interpreter* (Lowey Institute, publisher) https://www.lowyinstitute.org/the-interpreter/french-australian-submarine-deal-broader-political-and-strategic-context-mattered

Tillett, A. (2021, May 14). New pressures emerge in French submarine fight. *Australian Financial Review.* https://www.afr.com/politics/federal/new-pressures-emerge-in-french-submarine-fight-20210513-p57rid.

Tomkins, R. (2016, April 26). DCNS picked to design Australian submarines. United Press International, https://www.upi.com/Defense-News/2016/04/26/DCNS-picked-to-design-Australian-submarines/6521461683491/

White, H. (2020, March 18). Australia's Attack-class submarines need competition. *The Strategist*. https://www.aspistrategist.org.au/australias-attack-class-submarines-need-competition/

Woolner, D., & Glynne-Jones, D. (2019, July 22). Future-proofing the Attack class (part 3): regional superiority. *The Strategist*. https://www.aspistrategist.org.au/future-proofing-the-attack-class-part-3-regional-superiority/

CASE STUDY 10

"Tell 'him he's dreamin'"
The Olympic Games - a case of over-promising and under-delivering.

David Gration

Introduction

The Olympic Games can be described as a 'mega event' which Getz (2012) defines as "by way of their size or significance, are those that yield extraordinary high levels of tourism, media coverage, prestige or economic impact for the host community, venue or organisation." They are a magnet for idealists, opportunists and politicians. Big budgets and even bigger promises seem to be magnetically drawn to them. Events such as the Olympic Games provide an ideal breeding ground for White Elephants with their often-grandiose predictions of great benefits. Over-promising and under-delivering.

This case study will briefly look at the historical origins of the ancient and modern Olympic Games. The staging objectives of both the IOC and Host/Bidders will be outlined. Some examples of significant typical white elephant projects in the modern Olympic era will be described before focusing on Australia as a past (Melbourne, 1954 and Sydney, 2000) and future (Brisbane, 2032) Olympic Games host.

Short history of the development of the Olympic Games

The ancient Olympic Games covered the period from 776BC (in Olympia) until the last of the regular Games being held in 261AD. The ancient Olympics were a celebration of Greek (Hellenic) culture that focused on religious ceremonies, physical skill prowess and festive celebration. The IOC website describes it as "At their heart, the Games were a religious festival and a good excuse for Greeks from all over the Mediterranean basin to gather for a riotous barbeque" (IOC, 2022A).

All Greek city-states were invited to send participants and were given unhindered travel rights to the Games site. While the objective of celebrating what it is to be part of "Hellas" has been widely accepted to have been achieved, it did not always result in pan-Hellas peace between the city-states of Hellas. Like many events the short-term goodwill did not always last long past the short delivery period of the event itself.

The modern Olympic Games were the brainchild of Pierre, baron de Coubertin, and were inaugurated in Athens in 1896 (Finley and Pleket, 2012). The International Olympic Committee (IOC) was founded 2-years earlier at the Sorbonne University in Paris on 23 June 1894 at the first ever Olympic Congress. Unlike the ancient Olympics the decision was taken not to have a single host site in Greece but to have the event staged every four years in a different city, to not be the ancient Olympic Games reborn but to become the modern 'internationalised' Olympic Games.

The IOC's current Mission is "To promote Olympism throughout the world and to lead the Olympic Movement. It also describes its role in sport in 18 statements which include an array of topics including the protection of athletes, the development of sport, combatting drugs in sport, the sustainability of the Olympics and ensuring the Games leave a positive legacy to host cities (IOC, 2022B).

From the IOC/host city interaction perspective there has been a major shift in how the candidacy and bidding processes will be managed in the future. This comes in the light of past charges of corrupt processes and the inability of many cities to be able to afford the increasing costs of staging (IOC, 2018).

Masterman (2014) noted that the 2014 IOC Session gave unanimous approval to Olympic Agenda 2020, providing the strategic direction for a major review of all aspects of organising the Olympic Games – from candidature to Games delivery through to legacy. This enabled a fresh rethink for how future Olympic Games could be organised. Of the 40 recommendations within Olympic Agenda 2020, six focused on aspects of the organisation of the Olympic Games;

1. Shape the bidding process as an invitation

2. Evaluate bid cities by assessing key opportunities and risks

3. Reduce the cost of bidding

4. Include sustainability in all aspects of the Olympic Games

12. Reduce the cost and reinforce the flexibility of Olympic Games management

13. Maximise synergies with Olympic Movement stakeholders

A primary aim was to simplify the Candidature Process and to create Games which were viable and fit for modern circumstances, unlocking more value for host cities that had been notably absent in many previous Games.

Th3 concluding statement in the report broke new ground for the IOC who had previously had no objectives focused on economic, physical facility or other legacy benefits for the Host City. Their focus had been primarily on IOC and member organisation outcomes, in other words 'are they capable of holding the event and how does this help us, with benefits to the Host city being secondary.'

Having summarised the history of the Olympic Games, both ancient and modern, and established the mission of the IOC and its current objectives in relation to improving their role in the staging of the Olympic Games we are left with a series of self-stated criteria on which IOC Games outcomes can be judged. The following section addresses the Olympic Games from the perspective of Bidders/Hosts to examine the motivations behind bids for Olympic Games and the potential conflicts and boosterism that can occur.

Host Cities

Bidding for the Olympics is a daunting and costly process. A potential host city must convince the IOC that it has what it takes to financially and physically meet the needs of successfully staging an Olympic Games. That it is the best option to meet the needs of the international Olympic movement and its constituent sporting bodies. In assessing the potential hosts the bidders are visited by the Future Host Commission of the International Olympic Committee to assess the ability of the host city to deliver on its proposal. This process creates enormous pressure, and expenses, on applicant cities to impress and convince the Commission. They are trying to meet the IOC selection criteria on areas such as venues, transportation, environmental sustainability, marketing plans and evidence of financial capability etc. These need to be documented as part of the case for selection and proof of why they are the best bid. Like poker players the cards held by other bidders contain many unknowns.

According to the McBride and Manno (2021) "Cities invest millions of dollars in evaluating, preparing, and submitting a bid to the IOC. The cost of planning, hiring consultants, organizing events, and the necessary travel consistently falls between $50 million and $100 million. Tokyo spent as much as $150 million on its failed 2016 bid, and about half that much for its successful 2020 bid, while Toronto decided it could not afford the $60 million it would have needed for a 2024 bid."

Chicago spent up to US$100 million on its unsuccessful application to host the 2016 Games (Pletz, 2010). The British Government originally estimated that for London the cost of simply mounting a bid - and losing - would be around £17million. Earlier estimates from the London Assembly (2003, p. 7) showed that on current estimations, the total cost of bidding for the 2012 Olympics is likely to be £13 million (of which £6 million would be funded by the public sector). Total cost for bidding, staging the Games, building facilities and purchasing land would be £1.8 billion. ... with most of the direct cost of the Olympics is borne by the public sector - the benefits tend to accrue directly to the private sector and only indirectly to the public purse."

Baade & Matheson (2016) summarise the situation as the host cities being responsible for the entire bill for organizing the Olympic Games with only a small proportion coming from the International Olympic Committee to help defray the costs. Costs include the "three major categories of general infrastructure such as transportation and housing to accommodate athletes and fans; specific sports infrastructure required for competition venues; and operational costs, including general administration as well as the opening and closing ceremony and security" (p. 202). They also identified three potential benefits for the host city being: "the short-run benefits of tourist spending during the Games; the long-run benefits or the "Olympic legacy" which might include improvements in infrastructure and increased trade, foreign investment, or tourism after the Games; and intangible benefits such as the "feel-good effect" or civic pride" (p. 202).

Host Cities are often driven to 'go for the gold' by a number of key players. Businesses seek economic gain through new contracts, politicians seek positive exposure and improved re-election prospects, the administrators of sporting organisations seek to promote their membership and the public seeks to enjoy the biggest show in the world – the modern Circus Maximus. Many of these proponents, as well as non-participant citizens, are often left disappointed, a case of over-promising and under-delivering.

A history of Olympic sized disappointments

As the modern Olympics grew they have moved from being highly desirable in terms of Host City benefit to being a potential Trojan Horse whose attractive looking benefits also encompassed large costs and potentially significant risks of negative outcomes. As stated by McCarthy (2021) "In the second half of the twentieth century, both the costs of hosting and the revenue produced by the spectacle grew rapidly, sparking controversy over the burdens host countries shouldered. A growing number of economists argue that the benefits of hosting the games are at best exaggerated and at worst non-existent, leaving many host countries with large debts and maintenance liabilities. Instead, many argue, Olympic committees should reform the bidding and selection process to incentivize realistic budget planning, increase transparency, and promote sustainable investments that serve the public interest."

The promises of Olympic Games bonanzas for hosts do not hold up in terms of economic benefits. A wide range of researchers (e.g. Fowler & Meichtry, (2008); McBride & Manno, 2021; McCarthy, 2021; von Rekowsky, 2013; Wagg, 2016; and Zimbalist, 2015) identified the following examples of poor outcomes:

Montreal, 1976: Worker strikes, mismanagement, and huge cost overruns (est. 720% cost over-run) left the city with $1.5 billion of debt that took 30 years to erase.

Barcelona, 1992: The Barcelona Olympics left the central Spanish government $4 billion in debt (est. 266% cost over-run), and the city and provincial governments an additional $2.1 billion in the red.

Nagano, 1998: The full cost of the Nagano Olympics will never be known, because the documents accounting for money spent on the Olympic bid were burnt on the orders of Nagano's Olympic Committee vice-secretary general. Yet it is clear it went vastly over budget and, as a result, Nagano fell into recession.

Sydney, 2000: The Auditor General of NSW estimated the Games' true long-term debt was $2.2 billion. Pre-Olympics, Australian officials estimated that tourism would quadruple after the Games, but there was no boost at all.

Athens, 2004: The Athens Olympics vastly exceeded its $4.6 billion budget. Many believe the real accrued debt of roughly $15 billion contributed to Greece's present financial crisis.

Beijing (2008): Broke all spending records with an estimated bill of US$50 billion. Many elaborate venues such as the 'Birds Nest' have not achieved the hoped for legacy outcomes. In Beijing, few details were spared. Along Jing Shun Lu, a formerly dusty road in the capital's suburbs, the government spent $30 million for an Olympics facelift, including trees, flowers and an ornamental wall. The road is a secondary access route to the city's airport, and near the rowing venue. People who used to live along the road were given a small sum in compensation and forced to move.

London 2012: Had a bill of just under $15 billion, 76% overbudget. The promised tourism and economic boom did not eventuate.

Rio de Janeiro 2016: (est. US$14billion - 352% cost overrun). The bid was made at a time of economic buoyancy and delivered at a time of economic stress for Brazil. Corruption was rampant and large-scale protest rioting took place. "At another time or in another country, the Games might have been different, but not here and not now," says University of São Paulo professor and long-time Olympic analyst Katia Rubio. "We climbed that initial roller-coaster ramp and took that big dive, but, in the end, there was nothing else. It was a big boost that ultimately led to nothing" (Drehs & Lajolo, 2017).

Tokyo 2020/21: Th original bid committee estimate for the Games was US$7 billion (2013). The 2020, COVID-19 (Coronavirus Disease 2019), postponement alone added US$2.8 billion to the budget. Japan's National Audit board reported the final cost id likely to be more than US$22 billion. Nikkei and Asahi (newspapers) estimated it as up to US$28 billion. This situation highlights the ongoing debate over the risks, costs and benefits of hosting the Olympic Games, especially after the ongoing COVID-19 pandemic forced a year's delay and sparked public opposition over going ahead with the festivities during a major outbreak.

According to Flyvbjerg et al. (2016, p. 2) "At 156 percent in real terms, the Olympics have the highest average cost overrun of any type of mega-project. Moreover, cost overrun is found in all Games, without exception; for no other type of mega-project is this the case. 47 percent of Games have cost overruns above 100 percent." Huge public debt, resident dislocation and other negative impacts are seen in many of the above examples. A recurring theme is the under-utilised and decaying facilities (stadia, athlete villages etc.), purpose-built for the Games, that can be seen in Host Cities such as in Sarajevo, Athens, Beijing and Rio to name a few. These are the evidence of failed planning, the white elephants left behind by the Olympic Games juggernaut. What then do Australian Host City experiences of past and future have to teach us?

The Australian Olympic Games

Australia has hosted two Olympic Games, being Melbourne (1956) and Sydney (2000). It has also successfully bid for the 2032 Olympic Games to be staged in Brisbane. With 3 successful bids Australia will be equalled by only a handful of other countries

Melbourne 1956 "The Friendly Games"

'I think we should busy ourselves trying to get the Games for Melbourne. We can organise them later'. This is a quote from the aptly named Lord Mayor of Melbourne, Sir James Disney (Cahill, 1989).

In June 1954 Melbourne won the right, over Argentina and Buenos Aires, to be Host City for the 16th Modern Olympic Games in 1956.This made Melbourne the first Host City outside of Western Europe and America (Coe, 2012). Melbourne set up a bid committee similar to that of the successful Los Angeles bid committee – a business "booster" group. The final bid document was a "deluxe propaganda volume bound in Merino fleece". A few critics of the time claimed it would be a "white elephant" and a financial burden without the support of professional sport and income from gambling.

Having won the bid, the arguing continued. Prominent sports identities such as Fred Lester publically bemoaned the sordid manoeuvrings around the selection of Olympic Games sites and the money-hungry litany of corrupt practices and capitalism (Cahill, 1989).

Given the lack of experience in Australia for staging major events the IOC kept close tabs on the preparations and in particular venues and athlete village facilities. After much factional fighting between supporters of a new RAS venue and the existing Melbourne Cricket Ground, the MCG was designated as the main Games venue. It was all about the funding, both the Victorian and Australian governments were tight for cash and feared a public backlash when there were many other needs that the community desired more. When IOC President Avery Brundage arrived in 1955 he demanded to know that given the promises that everything would be completed on time how, in light of the inaction and dissention of the previous six years, could he be sure of delivery "Will it be done?" Cahill (1989).

The People's Republic of China refused to send a team as Chinese Taipei (Republic of China) had accepted an invitation to compete, an issue which continues to this day in various forms. The Australian Olympic Committee (AOC) tried unsuccessfully to sell international broadcasting rights. This had never been attempted for any previous Games. For future Host Cities and the IOC, the sale of international broadcasting rights has become a core source of funding.

The Melbourne Olympic Games while anecdotally successful and leaving strong sporting legacies was also one that was built on unfulfilled promises for many of its early proponents. The estimated final operating budget of A£5,400,000 and A£8,000,000 far exceeding earlier bid budget estimates. Two quotes from the Melbourne Olympics official report (1956) from the 1956 Olympic Games Organising Committee are worthy of consideration:

Calm judgment, of course, indicates that in some ways the effect of such great athletic events is relatively ephemeral. I for one would make no extravagant claims about them. But long after the names of the winners have faded from memory and the records then made have been broken, there will remain in the minds of many thousands of men and women, old or growing old, a warming memory of an event which had, as I believe, an enduring human significance. Hon. Robert Menzies, Prime Minister of Australia (p. 14)

And

The outlay on the Games in Melbourne is estimated at some £8,000,000. The Olympic ideal, however, does not reckon with profit and loss. They are less than nothing compared with the dividends in goodwill, not only in sport, not only for Melbourne or Australia, rich though this may be, but indestructibly in the hearts of men and women there and everywhere.

Edward A. Doyle, Honorary Editor (p. 24)

The Melbourne Games undoubtedly built momentum for rival Australian capital cities to bid. Australia was proved capable of winning and staging a major international event and arch rival Sydney was not to be outdone.

Sydney 2000 – "The Millennium Games"

During the 80's Australia's desire to host another Olympic Games was growing. The competition both between Australian cities and other international bidders had begun. Brisbane failed in its bid for the 1992 Summer Olympics, Melbourne failed in its bid for the 1996 Summer Olympics. In 1991 The AOC set about the creation of a Sydney bid for the year 2000. The bid was based on being 'greener' and 'friendlier' and an ideal time to show 'the Olympic Flame' in the fast-growing Asia-Pacific region. Despite strong international city competition at the IOC meeting on September 23, 1996 the winner was 'Syd-en-ey'.

The Sydney Organising Committee for the Olympic Games (SOCOG) budgeted A$2.3 billion to run the Games, including approx. A$675 million for venues and athlete villages at a re-envisaged, and chemically detoxed, Homebush Bay precinct. In addition to this the NSW and Australian government contributed approx. A$4 billion towards transportation projects such as road and train upgrades and a sparkly new monorail linking the Sydney CBD and Homebush Olympic village. Major legislation was introduced by both the Australian and NSW governments to facilitate and protect the Olympic Games in the areas of security powers for police, protection for Games sponsors from ambush marketing and environmental 'green enforcement' powers. Some of these additional powers lingered long after the Sydney Games were over.

According to Preuß et al. (2019) cost estimates varied between presented publically by the NSW government and SOCOG. "The government did not release the true costs expected, even though it knew at least that costs were higher than announced, which is a typical index of the winner's curse during the bidding process, as the backing of the population is important. While according to the neo-institutionalist PRINCIPAL-AGENT theory, this situation is called "adverse selection". The bidders (the government and the OCA), which are the AGENTS, have an incentive not to provide full information (playing with information asymmetry) to the PRINCIPAL (taxpayers) in order to increase their probability of winning the bid (opportunistic behaviour of the AGENT)" (p. 46). Upon this type of 'smoke and mirrors' are the seeds of disappointment sown. "The cost of the Sydney Games steadily rose from initial budget estimates. Initial slow ticket sales and the failure to meet sponsorship targets necessitated budget cuts and an injection of additional funds from the New South Wales Government" (Haynes, 2000, p. 4).

Successes related to the Sydney Olympics were built upon strong stakeholder management and communications. Malfas (2003) argued that although the IOC has final responsibility for the Olympic Games, it delegates most of the work to the relevant Host City OCOGs, which is highly reliant on government and commercial partners to deliver an Olympic Games (Malfas, 2003). As a result of this limited involvement by the IOC, as the parent organisation of the mega-sport event project, the loose organisational model provides opportunities for stronger stakeholders to strategically maximise their interests (Frawley, 2011). Stakeholders of mega events can prove to be a combination of 'blessings and curses'.

Bid organisers, like Sydney Olympic Games bid committee, often over-bake the projected outcomes for stakeholders in order to win the 'cherished prize of hosting the world's largest event that would leave in its wake a great legacy for the public benefit. This over-estimation of benefits creates a customer/stakeholder Expectation Gap (Barney, 2006). Poor facility usage, budget over-runs and a failed monorail are among the white elephant legacies from the

2000 Sydney Olympics.

Having examined the 2 previous Australian Olympic Games hosts we now turn our gaze to the future, the 2032 Brisbane Olympic Games.

Brisbane 2032

On the first day of competition in Tokyo, the International Olympic Committee (IOC) awarded the Games of the 35th Olympiad in 2032 to Brisbane. It was a Steven "Bradbury" moment with Brisbane being the last Bidder remaining. "Brisbane 2032 is the first future host to have been elected under, and to have fully benefited from, the new flexible approach to electing Olympic hosts," IOC president Thomas Bach said in a press release. "The reforms enable the IOC to work in partnership with cities, regions, and countries, to encourage Olympic projects which use a high percentage of existing and temporary venues, which align with long-term development plans, and which have a strong vision for sports and local communities" (IOC, 2021). This makes Brisbane the Test Case for the new way the IOC interacts with bidders and the successful Host City. Time will tell if it is successful for all the stakeholders.

One Prediction

In discussing *How will hosting the Olympic Games in 2032 benefit Brisbane?* Assoc. Professor Sarah Kelly of the UQ Business School, Faculty of Business, Economics and Law ventured to predict the following for the Brisbane Games in 2032:

"A successful 2032 Olympics bid would produce extensive, measurable, social and economic impacts for Brisbane, Queensland and the nation. Significant impacts include bringing forward key infrastructure planned for the longer term, such as more efficient transport, community gentrification, enhanced health and security, and improved sporting and event venues. Diplomatic and trade soft power would be advanced through promoting Queensland's destination image as safe and politically stable. A mega sporting event provides a platform to leverage and grow local technology to support infrastructure and services, which directly benefits the economy. Community pride and connection will also be enhanced, especially if local business and residents are actively involved in co-creating the event. Business and government partnerships are also expected to grow and strengthen by uniting around a common mission, centred upon generation of positive economic impact. Hosting the Games could also force governments into longer-term planning, resulting in broader social goals aimed at sustainability, equity and diversity" (UQ Contact Magazine, 2022).

The above is a great summary and it is hoped that many academic researchers will be tracking and measuring both the success and the failures of the Games. It is also hoped that a longitudinal cost-benefit analysis is undertaken.

The Brisbane 2032 Bid

Since the announcement of Brisbane being the winning city to host the 2032 Olympic Games, numerous documents have been published detailing the Brisbane bid as well as supporting documents from various government agencies. Additionally, the Queensland Government has passed legislation detailing the structure of the Olympic management organisation.

IOC – Brisbane Bid document

The IOC Future Host Commission Questionnaire Response final submission - May 2021 is a 98-page report responding to the requirements of the IOC committee in charge of bids for

Host Cities. The document can be found on the IOC website (AOC, 2021). In budgetary terms Revenue has been estimated at A$4,941,772,000 and Expenditure at the exact same figure of A$4,941,772,000. This means the net financial result will be A$0, an amazing achievement or wishful thinking, only time will tell. It should be noted that contributions from host governments have not been included and there are some glaring expenditure requirements unbudgeted in this report.

Australian Government – Report

Following a successful IOC feasibility assessment (IOC 2021B) on 24 February 2021, the International Olympic Committee entered into exclusive negotiations with the Queensland Government to host the 2032 Olympic Games. The Commonwealth Government subsequently committed to fund half the costs of critical infrastructure.

"This may include sports-related infrastructure, such as competition venues, Olympic villages, an international broadcast centre and a media and press centre, and non-sports-related infrastructure, such as transport infrastructure that is needed for the Games but is not directly related to staging the Games. This appears to be a greater funding commitment, in proportional terms, than occurred for the Sydney Games in 2000. The Commonwealth has also given the IOC guarantees about provision of government services in support of Brisbane's bid. Following the release of the 2021/22 Budget, media sources suggested the Commonwealth Government would spend between A$5.8 billion and A$6.0 billion on critical infrastructure in Queensland over the next decade if the Brisbane Games go ahead. The Budget papers, however do not contain any committed spending. This may be because the timing and magnitude of funding is uncertain and beyond the forward estimates" (Australian Government, 2021).

Queensland Government (2022) Legacy Program

"Brisbane 2032 aspires to create a lasting social, economic and environmental legacy. Our vision is to capitalise on sport and Brisbane 2032 as agents for positive change through a legacy-led approach that will drive benefits for the next 20 years and beyond. Brisbane 2032 will help accelerate long-term state-wide and regional priorities and will provide a national platform to amplify everything from healthy and active community initiatives to arts and culture, sustainability initiatives, tourism, trade and business development opportunities.

As part of Queensland's submission to the International Olympic Committee in 2021, initial legacy opportunities were identified as follows:

1. Sport and healthy lifestyle pathways.
2. Human skills, networks and innovation.
3. Culture and creative development.
4. Environmental benefits and targets.
5. Economic benefits.

The Brisbane 2032 Legacy Strategy will be delivered in partnership across all levels of government, industry and the community to achieve optimal legacy outcomes over the next 20 years and beyond. Games partners will work together to refine the legacy vision for Brisbane 2032 prior to broader industry and community engagement in 2022" (Qld. Govt., 2021). Many of these are broad legacy objectives with little in the way of detailed supporting documentation. Promises that, if history holds true, will fall short.

The Council of Mayors (SE Queensland)

In 2015 the Council of Mayors (SEQ) began investigating a regional Olympic and Paralympic Games proposal as a catalyst to expedite infrastructure delivery to support our growing region and to boost the economy and significantly raise the region's profile on the international stage.

Recognising that connectivity is the lifeblood of SEQ and its economy, the region's Mayors were committed to investigating how the Olympic and Paralympic Games could leave a positive legacy for the region by accelerating the funding and delivery of major infrastructure for the future of SEQ.

Council of Mayors (SEQ) Director and Sunshine Coast Council Mayor Mark Jamieson said the Olympic and Paralympic Games presented a significant opportunity to supercharge the south-east and Queensland's recovery from the COVID-19 pandemic.

The SEQ Mayors embarked on this journey to accelerate infrastructure investment, boost job creation, and attract tourism and investment to South East Queensland.

"These economic drivers, partnered with the International Olympic Committee's ongoing cost reforms, make the 2032 Games a compelling proposition for Queensland.

"We have always seen the potential to host the Olympic and Paralympic Games as a means to open up a wealth of opportunities for Queensland through pre-Games training, business and procurement opportunities, tourism and global exposure," said Mayor Jamieson." Around the Rings (2021). The inclusion of this diverse range of local governments with the other levels of government creates both opportunities and avenues for disagreement and feelings of 'we didn't get our fair share' from these stakeholders. Even 10 years out some 'gamesmanship' between LGA's over hosting venue rights has become evident.

Stakeholders - *Brisbane Olympic and Paralympic Games Arrangements Bill 2021*

The Palaszczuk Government (Queensland, 2021) passed historic legislation to establish an organising committee for Australia's most anticipated sporting event – the Brisbane 2032 Olympic and Paralympic Games.

Premier Palaszczuk announced that they had "… passed this important legislation to kickstart planning for Brisbane 2032 and lay the foundations for the $8.1 billion uplift the Games will deliver," the Premier said. "Over the next decade, the OCOG will continue to collaborate with Games partners, including the International Olympic and Paralympic committees, the Australian Olympic Committee and Paralympics Australia, and three tiers of Government.

The Organising Committee will be responsible for some of the most memorable moments of the Games – from triumphant torch relays, to an inspiring opening ceremony and a showstopping closing ceremony at no cost to the tax payer. The International Olympic Committee and private commercial revenue, including domestic sponsorship, ticket sales and merchandise will ensure all activities associated with the organising committee are delivered on a cost-neutral basis. It will engage thousands of enthusiastic Queenslanders to be Games volunteers, and undertake an enormous logistical feat, arranging accommodation and transport for tens of thousands of competitors, officials and media."

"I know the Organising Committee will deliver an unforgettable and unifying Games for Queensland, Australia and the world. The Organising Committee will operate as an independent statutory body, with a Board of Directors overseeing its effective and efficient operation."

Background:

The Bill provides that the Board will be made up of the following:

- five independent directors nominated by the Minister, with the consent of the Prime Minister (with one being the President)
- up to four persons nominated by the Prime Minister
- four persons nominated by the Premier

- one person nominated by the Lord Mayor
- the Lord Mayor
- the President or Honorary Life President of the Australian Olympic Committee (AOC)
- the President of Paralympics Australia (PA)
- any active members of the International Olympic Committee (IOC) residing in Australia
- any members of the International Paralympic Committee (IPC) Governing Board residing in Australia
- the chief executive officer of the AOC
- a recent Olympic athlete as confirmed by the AOC Athletes' Commission
- a recent Paralympic Athlete as confirmed by the PA Athletes' Commission." Queensland Government (2021)

The range of stakeholders for the 2032 Games will be much more extensive than those on the above Organising Committee membership. Stakeholders will be numerous including many international governments and national sporting bodies, construction and services groups, a wide range of public service organisations, the media, tourism & transport representative, Australian police and military services, Games volunteers etc. No-one should forget that the Australian taxpayers and residents who will bear the burden of any financial or /organisational/ service delivery errors in the lead-up to and during the Games, and potentially for years after the Closing Ceremony.

As a future Olympic Games, Brisbane 2032 provides an ideal opportunity to identify key decision-making and achievement milestones, and track if the plan is on-track and relevant. Will Brisbane 2032 organisers avoid the traps identified by Vincent (2019) of unforeseen delays, over promising of benefits, scope changes and the "eternal beginner" syndrome? Do you hear the herd stampeding in the distance?

Conclusions

How then should we judge the Olympic Games in terms of being a "White Elephant"? The Games are large and extremely complex projects with many stakeholders having a wide range of sometimes conflicting agendas. Part sporting extravaganza, part nationalistic boosterism, part celebration/party and part economic money-maker for some stakeholders. Given the findings of the many previous Olympic Games post-event assessments it would be wise if local hosts for the 2032 Games were careful to avoid over-promising and subsequent under-delivering.

There are some critical questions to be answered when considering bidding for events of the magnitude of the Olympic Games"

- WHY should we do it? (at every stage ask Why/ Why? Why?)
- WHAT information is critical in order to make an informed decision and can we access it?
- WHO are the beneficiaries and WHY do they deserve it?
- WHO are the key stakeholders and how can we bring them into partnership?
- WHAT are the opportunity costs related to the expenditure public funds?
- WHAT resources do we have to make it happen and are they accessible?
- WHO will pay for it?
- HOW do we compare with other bids in terms of existing facilities and other competitive advantages?
- WHEN is the right time to bid/hold the Games and can we make the timeline work?
- WHAT are the risks and HOW will they be managed?

If you can't find satisfactory answers for the above then, like Darryl Kerrigan (Michael Caton) in the 1997 Australian film The Castle, *"Tell 'him he's Dreamin"* and you will avoid that potential herd of Olympic size White Elephants.

Note:

The Board of the Brisbane Organising Committee for 2032 Olympic and Paralympic Games was announced in April 2022. This included a number of OG and AOG Administrative Officers, Australian Local, State and Commonwealth representatives, Sporting and Business identities. One month later, following the Australian Government Commonwealth election, changes to the board membership were already happening. One month down and counting.

References

Around the Rings (2021, July). *Council of Mayors (SEQ) Media Release - Brisbane 2032 named "preferred host" for Games.* INFOBAE. https://www.infobae.com/aroundtherings/federations/2021/07/12/council-of-mayors-seq-media-release-brisbane-2032-named-preferred-host-for-games/

Australian Government (2021) Budget Review 2020/21, Brisbane Olympic Games 2032 https://www.aph.gov.au/About_Parliament/Parliamentary_Departments/Parliamentary_Library/pubs/rp/BudgetReview202122/BrisbaneOlympicGames2032

Australian Olympic Commission (2021). IOC Future Host Commission Questionnaire Response. https://stillmed.olympics.com/mediaDocuments/International-Olympic-Committee/Commissions/Future-host-commission/The-Games-of-The-Olympiad/Brisbane-2032-FHC-Questionnaire-Response.pdf?_ga=2.143093168.400459524.1627282108-1934078332.1620901465

Baade, R. A., & Matheson, V. A. (2016). Going for the gold: The economics of the Olympics. *Journal of Economic Perspectives, 30*(2), 201-18. https://pubs.aeaweb.org/doi/pdfplus/10.1257/jep.30.2.201

Barney, R. K. (2006). The Bitter-Sweet Awakening: The Legacy of the Sydney 2000 Olympic Games. *Olympika: The International Journal of Olympic Studies, 15,* 129+. https://link.gale.com/apps/doc/A175877034/

AONE?u=anon~a136545b&sid=googleScholar&xid=bae12fc6

Cahill, S. (1989). *The Friendly Games? The Melbourne Olympic Games in Australian Culture 1946-1956.* University of Melbourne. https://minerva-access. unimelb.edu.au/bitstream/handle/11343/39429/72384_00000652_02_Part1. pdf?sequence=2&isAllowed=y

Coe, B. (2012). Olympic Games of 1956 (Melbourne) in J. Nauright (Ed.). *Sports around the World: History, Culture, and Practice [4 volumes]: History, Culture, and Practice.* (pp. 223–225) Abc-Clio.

Drehs, W. and Lajolo, M. (2017, Oct. 8): *After the Flame.* ESPN. https://www. espn.com/espn/feature/story/_/id/20292414/the-reality-post-olympic-rio

Finley, M. I., & Pleket, H. W. (2012). *The Olympic Games: the first thousand years.* Courier Corporation.

Flyvbjerg, B., Stewart, A., & Budzier, A. (2016). *The Oxford Olympics Study 2016: Cost and cost overrun at the games.* arXiv preprint arXiv:1607.04484. *https://arxiv.org/ftp/arxiv/papers/1607/1607.04484.pdf*

Fowler G. and Meichtry, S. (2008, July 16). China Counts the Cost of Hosting the Olympics, *Wall Street Journal.* https://www.wsj.com/articles/ SB121614671139755287

Frawley, S. (2011). *Organising Sport at the Olympic Games: The Case Study of Sydney* (Doctoral dissertation, Griffith University).

Getz, Donald (2012). *Event studies: theory, research and policy for planned events.* 2nd ed. London, United Kingdom: Routledge.

Haynes, J. (2000). *Socio-economic impact of the Sydney 2000 Olympic Games.* Centre d'Estudis Olímpics (CEO-UAB). https://ddd.uab.cat/pub/ worpap/2000/hdl_2072_5007/WP094_eng.pdf

International Olympics Committee (2018) *Olympic Agenda 2020.* https:// stillmed.olympic.org/media/Document%20Library/OlympicOrg/ News/2018/02/2018-02-06-Olympic-Games-the-New-Norm-Report.pdf

International Olympics Committee (2021A). IOC elects Brisbane 2032 as Olympic and Paralympic host. https://olympics.com/ioc/news/ioc-elects-brisbane-2032-as-olympic-and-paralympic-host

IOC International Olympics Committee (2021B). Feasibility Assessment – Olympic Games Brisbane 2032. https://library.olympics.com/Default/doc/

SYRACUSE/620465/ioc-feasibility-assessment-olympic-games-brisbane-international-olympic-committee?_lg=en-GB

International Olympic Committee (2022A). *Welcome to the Ancient Olympic Games.* https://olympics.com/ioc/ancient-olympic-games)

International Olympic Committee (2022B). *Mission statement.* https://olympics.com/ioc/mission

London Assembly (2003): *London's Bid for the 2012 Olympic Games.* A report from the London Assembly's Culture, Sport and Tourism Committee. https://www.london.gov.uk/sites/default/files/gla_migrate_files_destination/archives/assembly-reports-culture-olympics.pdf

Malfas, M. (2003). *An analysis of the organisational configurations over the life cycle of the Sydney organising committee for the Olympic Games* (Doctoral dissertation, Loughborough University).

Masterman, G. (2014). *Strategic Sports Event Management.* Routledge.

McBride, J. and Manno, M. (2021, December 15). *The Economics of Hosting the Olympic Games.* Council on Foreign Relations. https://www.cfr.org/backgrounder/economics-hosting-olympic-games

McCarthy, N. (2021, July 21). *The massive costs behind the Olympic Games.* Forbes, https://www.forbes.com/sites/niallmccarthy/2021/07/21/the-massive-costs-behind-the-olympic-games-infographic/?sh=71a46ab446b0

Melbourne Olympics Official Report (1956). Official Report of the organising committee for the GAMES XVI OLYMPIAD MELBOURNE 1956. http://www.vrwc.org.au/tim-archive/articles/1956%20Olympics%20-%20Official%20LOC%20Report.pdf

Pletz, J. (2010). *Chicago 2016's final tally: $70.6 M spent on Olympics effort.* Crain's Chicago Business. https://www.chicagobusiness.com/article/20100517/NEWS02/200038265/chicago-2016-s-final-tally-70-6m-spent-on-olympics-effort

Preuß, H., Andreff, W., & Weitzmann, M. (2019). *Cost and revenue overruns of the Olympic Games 2000–2018.* Springer Nature. https://library.oapen.org/bitstream/handle/20.500.12657/23163/1006990.pdf?sequence=1

Queensland Government (2021, Dec. 2). Brisbane Olympic and Paralympic Games Arrangements Bill 2021. https://documents.parliament.

qld.gov.au/tableoffice/tabledpapers/2021/5721T1809.pdf?utm_
campaign=QLD&utm_source=hs_email&utm_medium=email&_
hsenc=p2ANqtz-9ka3q6YziG9HT3s5W-WhhaAWAJyYapblewxw0iDcTp
RZYmaFPaJ9jkILweW8BxKX-b3YkS

Queensland Government (2022). *Brisbane 2032 Olympic and Paralympic
Games Legacy Committee.* https://www.qld.gov.au/about/Brisbane2032/
legacy-program

UQ Contact Magazine (2022). *How will hosting the Olympic Games in 2032
benefit Brisbane?* Statement by Associate Professor Sarah Kelly. Retrieved
15 May, 2022. https://stories.uq.edu.au/contact-magazine/2021/how-will-
hosting-the-olympic-games-in-2032-benefit-brisbane/index.html

Vincent, T. (2019, May). How to explain Olympic Games cost overruns in
terms of Project Management 1, 2. PM World Journal *3(4).* https://
pmworldlibrary.net/wp-content/uploads/2019/05/pmwj81-May2019-
Vincent-how-to-explain-olympics-cost-overruns.pdf

Von Rekowsky, R. (2013). Are the Olympics a Golden Opportunity for
Investors. Leadership series, Investment Insights. *Fidelity Investments.*
https://www.fidelity.com/bin-public/060_www_fidelity_com/documents/
Are%20the%20Olympics%20a%20Golden%20Opportunity%20for%20
Investors_Fidelity.pdf

Wagg, S. (2016). *The London Olympics of 2012: Politics, promises and legacy.*
Springer.

Zimbalist, A. (2015). *Circus Maximus: The Economic Gamble Behind Hosting
the Olympics and the World Cup.* Brookings Institution Press. https://doi.
org/10.7864/j.ctt1287brp

Lessons from the stampede

Scott Prasser

Introduction

This concluding chapter reviews the key lessons from the ten case studies. In so doing it considers not just what these case studies tell us about their particular projects and policies, but asks the more fundamental question: why are there so many such projects and can the numbers be culled in the future, and the stampede slowed?

Of course, these examples are just the tip of the iceberg – or rather in keeping with the metaphor – merely the ones picked from the passing herd of white elephant projects. There were just so many from which to choose.

At the same time there is much in modern life Australia by both government and the private sector that is done well. We would not enjoy our current the level of prosperity, full employment, a national health system, and security and stability of our society that we presently do if that was not the case. That this has been done in Australia with less public spending and lower taxes, while delivering better outcomes for our citizens than many other countries suggest much is working well in this country.

Nevertheless, as the case studies suggest, there is room for improvement.

Of course, white elephant projects or government follies are not new. Barbara Tuchman in her famous book, *The March of Folly* relates how governments, from the ancient past to recent times, commit follies and act contrary to their own self-interest. Tuchman asked:

> Why do holders of high office so often act contrary to the way reason points and enlightened self-interest suggests? Why does intelligent mental process seem so often not to function? (Tuchman, 1975. p. 2)

This is the very question which all the case studies in this volume have asked and to which they have sought to answer.

What are white elephant projects and policies?

Just to recap – we need to remind ourselves just what are white elephant projects and why these case studies were included in this volume.

In summary, white elephant projects are defined in this volume as having the following characteristics:

First, they do not fully achieve their public stated objectives (sometimes objectives are either unstated, vague or muddled). Dollery's study of local government amalgamation (Case Study 4) highlights how despite all the promulgations, they rarely achieve their prime objective of reducing costs of local government administration.

Second, white elephant projects cost more than was promised or estimated. Almost all the case studies share this feature in varying degrees, but perhaps Case Study 9 on the recent submarine project best exemplifies this most unfortunate trait with projected costs constantly changing – and only in one direction – up.

Third, while white elephant projects might produce some marginal benefits, the issue is they never cover the project's real costs and more often end up costing more. Gration's study of previous Olympic Games (Case Study 10) warns how these events rarely meet their financial projections. Hooper's study of airports (Case Study 8) shows just how marginal many of these projects are even when the most ideal conditions are met.

Fourth, the other feature of white elephant projects is that they are too often maintained past their used-by date when it has long been clear that they are not working, are delivering sub-optimal results and are consuming too many resources. As Kellow reminds us in the Policy and Projects Overview, too many projects suffer from the classic 'sunk-costs' syndrome, whereby "poor choices will be persisted with, rather than abandoned" because of the level of resources and political reputations invested in a particular project. It is a case of throwing bad money, after bad. It is a matter of saving face and political reputation.

Fifth, we also agree with Tuchman in her definition of what constitutes a 'folly' such as the project must have been "perceived as counter-productive in its own time, not merely by hindsight" (Tuchman, 1975. p. 4). While many projects initially seem a good idea, it soon becomes evident that they were ill-conceived. The Milkshake video (our 'Dessert') to teach children about healthy consensual relationships was seen early to be flawed. Unusually, but fortunately, this project was abandoned sooner rather than later but some linger on too long (Dessert).

Sixth, there is a "feasible alternative course of action … available" (Tuchman, 1975). In other words, the project chosen was not the only alternative to tackle the problem. Schwartz points out in relation to *COVIDSafe* (Case Study 7) that there was alternative technology that might have been viable, but it was ruled out too quickly – partly as an attempt to increase uptake on the choice the government had already made and were unwilling to change. Kingston's analysis of the expensive, now almost defunct Queensland desalination plant developed by the Beattie Government in response to the then drought (Case Study 1) is an example where government rushed for a solution before properly assessing the nature, extent and duration of the problem – namely the drought. The drought broke and floods followed leaving one very big rusting white elephant on Queensland's Gold Coast.

Lastly, Tuchman argues that the decision to proceed with a policy or project "should be that of a group, not an individual ruler" (Tuchman, 1975). It is too easy for tyrants or dictators to overrule everyone and to proceed recklessly ahead with their favourite scheme. All the case studies involved some form of collective decision-making process in a democratic environment through political bodies like cabinet supported by advice from the public bureaucracy and usually with some form of parliamentary approval. Gration's study of the proposed 2032 Olympic Games (Case Study 10) highlights very well, that despite the multiple agencies, stakeholders, institutions, and levels of government involved in such projects in the past they proceed, and lessons are not always appreciated.

In general, projects which have gone astray because of unpredictable circumstances such as a natural disaster are not categorised as a white elephant project unless there was failure to consider, as a normal part of any proper risk analysis process, factors that contributed to the subsequent damage or loss. For instance, developing a new building without checking whether it was in a flood prone area and then was subsequently damaged by inundation can constitute a white elephant project.

One final point, while most of the examples in this volume are drawn from the public sector, Gary Banks reminds us that white elephant projects are not just a public sector phenomenon (Foreword). The private sector too, has indulged in mistakes that cost their shareholders greatly, and even led to many a firm's bankruptcy. The tourism industry in Queensland is full of examples of island resorts that have failed to deliver, went broke and were subsequently sold off at a fraction of their original costs. Car companies have produced their share of product failures that in some cases, like the 1957 Ford Edsel in the United States, almost broke the corporation. This model introduced with much hype, failed to sell as expected and was consequently discontinued after only a couple of years. It was Ford's 'white elephant' product.

Why should we be concerned?

In recent times, we have witnessed how in response to the pandemic, governments in Australia and elsewhere have increased spending to unprecedented levels. The acceptance of modern monetary theory (MMT) that overturned previous constraints about government spending contributed to justifying these large public expenditure increases than would previously have been unacceptable (Makin & Tunny, 2021). The underlying theme of MMT is that governments that issue their own currency cannot run out of money. Therefore, if a project fails this should not be a concern – just borrow some more and start again. Banks alerts us to these trends (Foreword).

While the costs of some white elephant projects in this collection are huge (Case Studies 8 and 9), others seem quite miniscule by comparison (Case Study 7 and 'dessert'). This does not mean we should not be concerned. After all, even these smaller projects consumed considerable resources in terms of both finances and staff time that could have been allocated more effectively elsewhere. They also distract attention from more important issues. The principle of opportunity costs applies here. More importantly, even when a project was originally established to respond to a real problem, their failure to perform satisfactorily means that issue was not addressed properly. For instance, the long running the Murray-Darling Basin Scheme (Case Study 2) shows that optimum results have not been achieved with consequential poor economic and environmental results. So, we all should be concerned about these white elephant failures – whether big or small, their costs, the misallocation of finite resources, and their policy failures.

Our other worry is that despite white elephant disasters being 'outed' by post evaluation processes through auditor-general, parliamentary committee reviews and even open public inquiries like royal commissions (see Queensland hospital payroll scandal Case Study 6) (Chesterman 2013) – white elephant projects continue to flourish as Commonwealth Auditor-General reports about defence procurement remind us again and again.

Causes

An important way to explain how white elephant projects occur is to distinguish between those caused by behavioural or human factors such as gross incompetence, groupthink, prejudice and bias and irrational thinking (Sutherland, 1992) and those that are "institutional, systemic or cultural in character" (King & Crewe. 2013, p. 7). While not denying the importance of individual behavioural drivers in causing disasters, accidents and white elephant projects, the case studies in this volume suggests that it is the institutional context in which individual and groups operate that is the more pivotal factor in causing white elephant projects to thrive.

For instance, a strong leader in a democracy might for reasons of personal pride, hubris or self-aggrandisement, want to pursue a particular project that has little public interest merit. It would be most likely to become a white elephant. However, in a democracy, the processes of collective decision making (cabinet, the public service), and a certain about openness (parliament, the opposition, role of the media, opinion polls, public consultation) would either stop the project or lead to some modifications that limit its adverse impacts. By contrast, in an autocratic regime or one-party state, a powerful leader can exercise complete power and claim adherence to the regime's ideology to justify a project regardless of its value.

Nevertheless, as Queensland's costly desalination plant shows (Case Study 1), how a strong leader even in a democracy, in this case Premier Peter Beattie, operating within a weak institutional setting (unicameral legislature, politicised public service and tight party discipline) (Tunny, 2018) overrode legitimate concerns about the proposed plant. This project also highlights another contributing factor that has become more evident in western democracies, namely that government is expected to 'do something' about almost every issue and that governments can 'fix' everything. The long drought in Queensland raised concerns about its impacts on the environment, the economy and the viability of some communities. It thus became an issue high on the political agenda. The desalination plant was 'the something' which the Beattie Government produced to meet the public demand for 'action'. It was a very costly response.

Market-economies should be less prone to producing white elephant projects as costs and benefits are more easily evaluated than in more ideologically driven non-market economies. However, the private sector and interest groups are often 'rent-seekers' procuring benefits in the form of government subsidies for activities for which there is no market and that produce limited public benefits. The Division 10BA amendments to the *Income Tax Assessment Act* (see Case Study 5) that permitted a 150 per cent tax write-off for investors in the local film industry is one example. It caused investment in projects that did not always come to fruition. Investment was made more to gain financial benefits for investors than to promote a local film industry. As the case study concluded, the scheme was "one of the most extravagant such benefits in the developed world." It was an expensive white elephant project. The same argument could be applied to major events like Olympic Games (Case Study 10) where costs are often downplayed and benefits exaggerated and projected long into the future.

By the way, there is also 'pork-barrelling' which although different from 'rent-seeking' shares certain common features. Pork barrelling is when a government seeks to gain electoral support from a particular group or locality by providing a subsidy, program or some type of infrastructure that has limited or no wider public benefit. The 10BA film tax concession could be seen as a vehicle to gain votes from the arts community. The multi-billion dollar SEA Future Submarine Program (Case Study 9) was to be based in Adelaide largely to secure seats for several federal coalition members, to gain support from a key Senate cross-bencher such as Adelaide based Senator Xenophon, and to assist a newly elected state Liberal government (Errington & Van Onselen, 2016, pp. 124-125).

Another explanation is that public projects are using other people's money – 'the taxpayers'. There is a disconnect between those who make decisions about projects, and the source of the funds. If cost overruns occur, it is only public money involved and therefore does not matter. More can always be found as MMT suggests. Redress is difficult as taxpayers are too amorphous a group to organise, protest and cause political damage to those responsible (Barber, 2015, pp. 151-179).

Some concerning trends as explanation

There are several recent trends and features of modern democracies that have nurtured the growth of white elephant projects. We are not saying that the past was a golden age in fiscal restraint, moral courage and public accountability. History, as Tuchman and others record, tells us otherwise.

First there has been in Australia, and in other western democracies, increasing politicisation of the public service, a loss of permanency for senior managers and thus a concomitant loss of continuity, expertise and independence. Governments get the advice they want rather than what they need.

Second, and related to these developments, has been organisational amnesia – the inability of organisations (and staff) to remember the successes and failures of the past. Not only are ministers (and their large and increasingly important ministerial staff) temporary, so too is the public service for reasons just discussed. Once the public service would know what worked and what did not. Now with such a high turnover of staff there has been a loss of memory (Pollitt, 2000, pp. 5-6; Tingle, 2015, pp. 1-86). Similar trends can be seen in the competitive private sector where there is a high turnover of senior management, boardroom coups, acquisitions and amalgamations and the inevitable restructurings and downsizing.

Third, democratic and competitive party politics is another factor. As Samuel Brittan correctly predicted in the 1970s that Keynesian economics provided a rationale for more public spending and the increased government involvement in society. Modern politics will just become a bidding war between political parties placing an ongoing upward pressure on public spending:

> The main point to stress is that democracy, viewed as a process
> of political competition, itself imparts a systematic upward

bias to expectations and compounds the other influences at
work. (Brittan, 1975, p. 141)

This bidding war between the major parties has been
accompanied by increasing public expectations on what
government can deliver and an all too willingness by
political parties and leaders to oblige. All this creates a fertile
environment for white elephant projects to flourish. Decision-
making is rushed - 'let's do it' rather than 'let's think about
it' dominates. The focus is short term – getting an immediate
'announceable' is the name of the game, especially in time for
the next election. Future costs and implementation strategies
can be worked out later. Also, there has been a tendency
for every emerging issue to be too easily labelled a 'crisis'
resulting in government (and media) overreactions, leading to
spending splurges, and initiating projects without due process
(Maor, 2012). Meeting media and public expectations in doing
something is the order of the day (see Case Study 7). Such
increasing government involvement into so many areas of
society prompted one commentator to ask "Can governments
become so overloaded with responsibilities that they could
not function properly?" (Starr, 1977). This is an issue that
elected governments are unwilling to admit, and the electorate
to acknowledge. It is one of the contributing factors for the
growth in the number of white elephant projects.

Suggestions for culling the herd

While highlighting the nature and extent of the white elephant
issue is important, this volume also explores how the problem
might be addressed. We do not expect to wipe out the herd
completely, but propose suggestions that might cull the
numbers and reduce the stampede to a gentle cantor so they
can be better corralled and managed. At the same time, we
appreciate this is not an easy task as the underlying causes
of white elephant projects – an expectation for government

to resolve everything and a lack of concern about spending increases and waste – have become so embedded in our political culture. Nevertheless, there must be a better way.

Certainly, starting with the obvious first, exhorting officials, CEOs, and politicians to "do better" or to exercise restraint, would be ineffective. Nor does relying on post evaluation processes like auditor-general reports and public inquiries the answer. They expose incompetence, waste and even systemic issues, but are too often forgotten and the lessons not learnt for reasons highlighted (see Case Studies 3 & 6). More importantly, it has been recognised that the origin of most white elephant projects lies in their design phase and a lack of concern about how they might be implemented. Decision makers need to appreciate that policy formulation is intimately related to implementation. This means more focus when developing a policy or project in clarifying what is feasible, cost-effective, and constitutionally and politically acceptable. As a former Commonwealth Auditor General observed:

> Policy implementation should be an integral part of policy design – begin with the end process in mind. This means engaging those with implementation experience during the policy development stage. This is important in assessing the practicality of a policy. (McPhee, 2007)

Without considering implementation and having clear goals, projects are too easily hijacked for other purposes distorting their original intentions resulting in project failure (Case Study 3).

A common theme of the case studies is what Hooper defines (Case Study 8) as the need for "better governance" which "requires accountability and transparency". Over and over, projects get started and are allowed to continue and grow to maturity because there is a deliberate, contrived vagueness about aims, costs and expectations. As a recent United Kingdom report by the Institute for Government on making policy better noted there was a need to resolve "who is accountable to whom, for what, and the mechanisms to achieve that accountability" (Hallsworth & Rutter, 2011). Flyvberg et al. in an much earlier international assessment of mega-projects placed a strong emphasis on improving accountability:

> ... good decision making is a question not only of better and more rational information and communications but also of institutional arrangements that promote accountability ... We see accountability as being a question not just about periodic elections, but also about a continuing dialogue between civil society and policy makers and about institutions holding each other accountable through appropriate checks and balances (Flyvbjerg, 2003, p. 7).

In Australia, the federal-state dimension exacerbates problems about what level of government is responsible for what and what the specific decision points are that determine success and prevents the birth of another white elephant project (Case Study 2). However, federalism and constitutional issues have to be managed and built into project design.

Then there is the issue of having good processes of decision making and policy development. As former Queensland senior public servants Peter Bridgman and Glyn Davis suggested:

> Experience shows that good process is integral to consistently good policy. While some very poor policies have grown out of the most rigorous process, it is rarer for good policy to grow from a haphazard approach. (Bridgmen et al., 1997, p. 27)

No-one disagrees, but it is easier said than done. All sorts of factors can lead to a good policy process and rational decision-making being bypassed – short term political exigencies, unexpected crises, and ideological commitments – and which can distort the very best of projects. The Adelaide submarine project (Case Study 9) had multi-processes but none meshed to provide the sense of direction the project needed. The Murray-Darling Basin project (Case Study 2) is entangled in a web of intergovernmental and stakeholder consultation processes, organisational politics and boundary conflicts. Governance is confused. Will the 2032 Brisbane Olympics, which also has an international dimension, become so entangled in processes (Case Study 10), that responsibility and accountability will be lost?

Care needs to be taken in prescribing more procedures or regulations as the means to policy salvation. More procedures and processes may make effective policy development redundant. The lament of many trying to develop new projects is the excessive processes and multi-agencies involved. They have not always led to better results.

Other suggestions such as to test projects before they are fully operationalised, by holding pilot programs, have long been used in some types of programs. They sometimes work. Often they are deployed by governments to show symbolic interest in an issue than to evaluate the appropriateness of future potential initiative.

Establishing new institutions is another way governments have sought to respond to new problems and to bring order to policy chaos. The public sector is littered with much heralded new bodies, only to see them wither away as political interest cools, another issue emerges or governments change. Nevertheless, Australia has pioneered some success stories. The Commonwealth's Productivity Commission with its legislated roles, extensive resources, open processes, perceived independence, clear methodology and quality of its reports, has been instrumental in helping governments initiate reforms across an array of areas (Stewart & Prasser, 2015). However, some contend, that in recent times the Productivity Commission has lost its influence and even some of its expertness. This may explain Australia's stagnation in productivity and the lack of clear government actions in this area (Kehoe, 2019). Dr Andrew Leigh, a federal Labor parliamentarian and frontbencher and an economist of some standing, has suggested creating the Office of an Evaluator General located in Treasury to "conduct high-quality evaluations" (Leigh, 2018) including randomised trials for projects before they start. A laudable objective, but exactly how this would work is unclear. Also, would a new body with such a threatening mission (possibly holding back new projects) really survive in the public bureaucracy and national politics?

Compounding the decline in 'expertness' within the public service for reasons discussed (Banks, 2012) has been the movement of decision making, advice and influence from the bureaucracy to ministerial offices. Experience and knowledge in these offices is often limited, their timeframes short, and their focus more on the politics than the policy (Maley, 2015). Little wonder white elephant projects have become so numerous.

Certainly, the other suggestion such as greater transparency concerning the full details of projects would, as several of the case studies suggest, make the public a little more concerned about their costs and encourage project leaders to be more sensitive to the effective management of projects. To improve transparency a greater role for parliament is often recommended. It is interesting to note how little parliament figures in much of the discussion in the ten case studies. That reflects a sad reality that parliament in our Westminster system is captured by the party with a majority – and hence the government of the day. In Australia, party loyalties are tight and partisanship strong. Even the Australian Senate's once highly regarded committees have increasingly become just another arena for partisan conflict. The 2022 Senate Committee review of the Morrison's Government's handling of the pandemic is an example. Dominated by opposition and minority party members, it found not one positive outcome.

This was regardless of Australian's better performance in many areas of managing the pandemic compared to other countries (Senate, 2022; Halligan & Reid, 2016). It was not a proper policy review about which there could have been legitimate criticisms, but rather was just a political witch-hunt providing no insights.

Conclusions

There are no magic solutions to addressing the white elephant stampede. Fortunately, the case studies in this volume, despite their dismal tales, do provide suggestions on how the problems they identified could have been addressed. In most cases there are suggestions about how their project could have been done differently and better. Alternatives could have been pursued and savings made. However, reform will not occur till the public demands more accountability, are outraged at the misallocation of resources and there is wider acceptance by all of us that resources are finite, and the effectiveness of government limited. Unless that happens, we just better get out of the way of the continuing and growing stampede of white elephants! They are coming your way.

References

Banks, G. (2012, July 3). *Public Inquires, Public Policy and the Public Interest*, Inaugural Peter Karmel Lecture in Public Policy, Academy of Social Sciences.

Barber, M. (2015). *How to run a government: So that citizens benefit and taxpayers don't go crazy.* Penguin UK.

Davis, G., Althaus, C., & Bridgman, P. (2012). *The Australian policy handbook.* Allen & Unwin.

Brittan, S. (1975). The economic contradictions of democracy. *British Journal of Political Science, 5*(2), 129-159.

Chesterman, R., & Queensland Department of Justice and Attorney-General (2013). *Queensland Health Payroll System Commission of Inquiry: Report*. Chair.

Errington, W., & Van Onselen, P. (2016). *The Turnbull Gamble*. Melbourne Univ. Publishing.

Flyvbjerg, B., Bruzelius, N., & Rothengatter, W. (2003). *Megaprojects and risk: An anatomy of ambition*. Cambridge university press.

Halligan, J., & Reid, R. (2016). Conflict and consensus in committees of the Australian parliament. *Parliamentary Affairs, 69*(2), 230-248.

Hallsworth, M., & Rutter, J. (2011). *Making policy better: Improving Whitehall's core business*. Institute for Government UK.

Kehoe, J. (2019, June 22). Dismal decade needs tax, IR fix: Banks. *Australian Financial Review*.

King, A., & Crewe, I. (2013). *The blunders of our governments*. Oneworld Publications.

Leigh, A., MP. (2018, Nov. 13). Building a better feedback loop: Labor to establish an evaluator general [Media Release].

Makin, T., & Tunny, G. (2021, May). The MMT Hoax. Centre for Independent Studies, Sydney, Policy Paper 41.

Maley, M. (2015). The policy work of Australian political staff. *International Journal of Public Administration, 38*(1), 46-55.

Maor, M. (2012). Policy overreaction. *Journal of Public Policy, 32*(3), 231-259.

McPhee, I. (2007). Foreword. In John Wanna (Ed.), *Improving Implementation: Organisational Change and Project Management* (p. xv), ANU E Press.

Pollitt, C. (2000). Institutional amnesia: A paradox of the 'Information Age'? *Prometheus, 18*(1), 5-16.

Senate Committee on COVID-19 (2022, April 7). Final report: *Senate select committee on COVID-19.* Australian Government.

Starr, G. (1977, May 7). Our overloaded governments. *Sydney Morning Herald.*

Stewart, J., & Prasser, S. (2015). Expert policy advisory bodies. In Brian Head and Kate Crowley, (Eds.), *Policy Analysis in Australia* (pp. 151-166). Policy Press.

Sutherland, S. (1992). *Irrationality: The enemy within.* Constable and Company.

Tingle, L. (2015). *Quarterly Essay Political amnesia: How we forgot how to govern* (Vol. 60). Black Inc.

Tuchman, B. W. (1975). *The march of folly: From Troy to Vietnam.* Abacus.

Tunny, G. (2018). *Beautiful One Day, Broke the Next: Queensland's Public Finances since Sir Joh and Sir Leo*, Connor Court Publishing.

Dessert

Discontent over Consent:
The Short Unhappy Life of the Milkshake Video

Steven Schwartz AM

ON 20 APRIL 2020, the federal government deleted several videos from its *Good Society* website. The clips were intended to teach children about healthy consensual relationships and sexual consent . A government spokesperson said the videos, which were only available for a short time, were removed from view in response to "community and stakeholder feedback." This was something of an understatement. A state education minister called one of the videos "cringeworthy" and a "big fail." Another minister described the same video as "woeful." Given that the budget for the *Good Society* website was $3.79 million, it is worthwhile delving more deeply into what went wrong.

Fortunately, printouts of relevant emails were reportedly found hidden in a taco box at Canberra Station. Their provenance cannot be determined; the emails may have been fabricated. Reach your own conclusions.

10 January

From: Corporate Optimisation Synthesist @Dept of 20th Century Skills, Generic Capabilities, Learning Progressions, and Education.gov.au

To: Chief Paradigm Analyst@Respect Matters.com.au

Subject: Good Society project

Hi Lileth,

I am writing to let you know that the government has appropriated $3.79 million to commission a "Good Society" website. The purpose of the website is to teach school-aged kids about sex, consent and relationships. I know you hoped for much more, but I trust you will be able to use this small amount to produce world-class educational resources suitable for teaching kids the true meaning of respect.

On a personal note, I believe the ideas you put forward are excellent. Re-interfacing the information superhighway so that our school children are at the cutting edge of the knowledge-based post-industrial paradigm is exactly what we want.

I have faith that you will step up to the plate, push the envelope and start to think outside the circle, square and box. We want the Good Society website to be innovative, seamless, borderless, inclusive and diverse as we go forward.

I am sure you understand,

Sam

Wisdom is our passion. Think before printing.

***

14 JANUARY

FROM: CHIEF PARADIGM ANALYST@RESPECT MATTERS.COM.AU

TO: OPTIMISATION DELIVERY TEAM@ RESPECT MATTERS.COM.AU

SUBJECT: CREATIVE IDEAS

Hi Team,

I hope you enjoyed the corporate wellness day, especially the ocean float meditation marathon. Mindfulness at sea was just what we needed to touch base, reset, and get the creative juices flowing. We will need all the visioning we can muster to produce world class videos for the *Good Society* website.

Imagineers, it is time to don your thinking caps and let me have content deliverables to help our younger generation learn to respect others, understand sexual consent, and develop healthy relationships.

Looking forward to your insights.

Lileth

MEETING STAKEHOLDER EXPECTATIONS.

THINK BEFORE PRINTING.

***

7 February

FROM: CHIEF PARADIGM ANALYST@RESPECT MATTERS.COM.AU

TO: OPTIMISATION DELIVERY TEAM@ RESPECT MATTERS.COM.AU

SUBJECT: Q AND A

Hi Team,

Come on Team. We have deadlines to meet, so let's have some game changing content. In the meantime, here are answers to your most common questions:

1. What impact are these videos expected to have?

   Answer: These videos will ensure that Australia is a good society. Watching the videos and discussing them in class will allow the younger generation to learn how to respect others, obtain consent for sexual activity and form nurturing relationships.

2. How will success be measured?

   Answer: Success will be measured by whether we get contracted to make more videos.

3. The Australian vernacular is new to me. Instead of "Can I touch your bum?" can I use American idioms such as "Can I touch your butt?" Does it matter if a video shows a briefcase full of American rather than Australian dollars, or whether our materials refer to "math "rather than "maths?"

   Answer: Don't worry. For a miserly $3.79 million, the government can't afford to be too picky. Besides, if anyone notices, we can always claim that these cross-cultural references are not errors, but a reflection of our commitment to cultural diversity.

I hope this answers your questions. Now, let's start visioneering.

Lileth

MEETING STAKEHOLDER EXPECTATIONS. THINK BEFORE PRINTING.

***

14 FEBRUARY

FROM: PRINCIPAL RESONANCE SPECIALIST@:PHOSPHORESCENCE STUDIOS

TO: CHIEF PARADIGM ANALYST@RESPECT MATTERS.COM.AU

SUBJECT: CONSENT VIDEO

I am a principal resonance specialist at Phosphorescence Studios. You may have seen some of my advertising work for Sticky Peanut Butter.

I have an out-of-the box idea for a sexual consent video that would resonate with young people.

Imagine a deconstructed *Happy Days* retro teen hangout. On one side of the set, there is a desk holding an old personal computer. On the other side, there is a wall of clunky old hi fi gear. Young people in flares are gathered around a pinball machine. A menu on the wall offers a peanut butter milkshake (an Aussie favorite, I hear).

A young couple are in the foreground. One is what most people would perceive to be a cis-gender male, the other a female. The female asks the male to taste her milkshake. He says he likes his own milkshake better. She responds by throwing the remainder of her milkshake in his face.

A sanctimonious narrator with a posh British accent explains that the female's behaviour has ethical and moral ramifications. Using a drawing of a rectangle with a moving vertical line, the narrator says throwing a milkshake in someone's face could move the line into the "end zone."

The cis-gender male believes his companion's behaviour reflects poorly on her and may even threaten their relationship. Initially, the female gloats but she ultimately comes to realise the error of her ways.

As you can see, the milkshake is a compelling metaphor. The take home message is the importance of ensuring appropriate consent for sex.

What do you think?

Harvey S

PHOSPHORESCENCE: LIGHT IN THE DARK.

THINK BEFORE PRINTING

***

21 February
FROM: CHIEF PARADIGM ANALYST@RESPECT MATTERS.COM.AU
TO: HARRY@REALJOB.COM
SUBJECT: I'LL BE HOME LATE

Sorry Harry, I'm going to have to miss dinner. I'll be home late. We need to get a sex video done ASAP and you'd never believe the moronic pitches I received. Milkshakes and tacos as metaphors for sex! I sent them to the usual suspects for advice. I thought they would laugh them away, but our education advisors seem to like them. (God, I regret my Communications Studies degree.)

Could you feed the kids?

Lxx

MEETING STAKEHOLDER EXPECTATIONS.
THINK BEFORE PRINTING.

***

1 APRIL

FROM: CHIEF PARADIGM ANALYST@RESPECT MATTERS.COM.AU

TO: OPTIMISATION DELIVERY TEAM@ RESPECT MATTERS.COM.AU

SUBJECT: GOING LIVE

Hi Team,

Today is the big day. (No not April Fool's day). Your video is going live. Let's be sure to share the credit. Remember there is no "I" in team.

Lileth

MEETING STAKEHOLDER EXPECTATIONS.

THINK BEFORE PRINTING.

***

2 APRIL

RADIO INTERVIEW WITH STUDENT:

WHAT DID YOU THINK OF THE MILKSHAKE VIDEO?

They must be like kidding, right? We want good jobs and that means we need to, like, learn how to do them, right? Anyway, how can you teach sex without at least, like, saying the word? Besides, everyone has a different idea of right or wrong. I may want to drink booze a lot and you might not. So, like, who's right then? See what I mean?

***

3 APRIL

FROM: CORPORATE OPTIMISATION SYNTHESIST @DEPT OF 20TH CENTURY SKILLS, GENERIC CAPABILITIES, LEARNING PROGRESSIONS, AND EDUCATION.GOV.AU

TO: CHIEF PARADIGM ANALYST@RESPECT MATTERS.COM.AU

SUBJECT: GOOD SOCIETY PROJECT

Dear Lileth,

I imagine you have now seen the comments on the "milkshake" video. These include "woeful'" "cringeworthy" and "6 minutes of WTF."

The department plans to withdraw the milkshake video (and the taco one) immediately. The department will announce that the videos were reviewed and approved by subject matter experts, but we always expected to keep materials fresh. We retired these videos as they went stale after a few days. Given your experience, we would welcome future applications from you as we plan further videos.

SAM

WISDOM IS OUR PASSION.

THINK BEFORE PRINTING.

***

ACRONYM INDEX

AFC – Australia Film Commission
ANAO – Australian National Audit Office
AOC – Australian Olympic Committee
ATAG – Air Transport Action Group
AUKUS – Australia, United Kingdom and USA
BANANA – build absolutely nothing anywhere near anybody
BAU – business as usual
CBA – cost benefit analysis
CBD – Central business district
CCSP – Collins Class Submarine Program
CGRC – Cootamundra Gundagai Regional Council
COAG – Council of Australian Governments
COVID-19 – Coronavirus Disease 2019
CRCFFI – Cooperative Research Centre for Future Farm Industries
CRCIA – Ciudad Real Central International Airport
CSIRO - Commonwealth Scientific and Industrial Research Organisation
ECA – European Court of Auditors
ERP – enterprise resource planning
ESC – Executive Steering Committee
ESP – Environment for Scheduling Personnel
EU – European Union
FBT – Fringe Benefits Tax
FSP – Future Submarine Program
GCCC – Gold Coast City Council
GCDP – Gold Coast Desalination Plant
ILGRP – Independent Local Government Review Panel
IOC – International Olympic Committee
IPC – International Paralympic Committee
IT – Information technology
ITP – Integrated Tree Processing
JVAP - Joint Venture Agroforestry Program
LGAQ – Local Government Association of Queensland
Lpd – Litres per day
MDBA – Murray Darling Basin Authority
MDBC – Murray Darling Basin Commission

ML - Megalitre
MRIA – Mattala Rajapaka International Airport
NIDA – National Institute for Dramatic Arts
NIMBY – Not in my backyard
NMI – National Water Initiative
NPA – National Partnership Agreement
NPWS – National Plan for Water Security
NSW – New South Wales
NT – Northern Territory
NWC – National Water Commission
OMA – Oil Mallee Association of WA
PA – Paralympics Committee
QH – Queensland Health
QLGRC – Queensland Local Government Reform Commission
QTC – Queensland Treasury Corporation
RAN – Royal Australian Navy
RFI – Request for Information
RIRDC – Rural Industries Research and Development Corporation
SAP – Systems Applications and Products
SDA – Solution Design Authority
SDL - Sustainable Diversion Limit
SEQ - South-East Queensland
TLM – The Living Murray
SEQ – South East Queensland
SOCOG – Sydney Organising Committee for the Olympic Games
SSA – Shared Service Agency
SSI – Shared Services Initiative
SSS – Size, Shape and Sustainability Initiative
TCorp – NSW Treasury Corporation
UK – United Kingdom
UNFCCC – United Nations Framework Convention on Climate Change
WA – Western Australia
WHO – World Health Organisation
WRP - Water Resource Plans

CASE STUDY QUESTIONS

The following sample of case study questions are aimed at encouraging the exploration of what causes *White Elephants* to occur and how they might be avoided, or at least minimised. The questions are suitable for group discussions, debates, assessments and to inspire further research.

CASE STUDIES

1. *'Water, water everywhere and not a drop to drink"* *The sad history of water politics in SE Qld and the bad politics that led to the 'solution' of desalination* by Bruce Kingston

QA. What role does NIMBY (not in my backyard) play in planning for major water infrastructure?

QB. How can long term benefits overcome short term political pain?

2. *Murray-Darling Basin Water Reforms – Money for Nothing and Water for Free* by Nadeem Samnakay

QA. Is there a magic formula for balancing Triple bottom Line with political imperatives?

QB. In this case study was there a single critical point at which the White Elephant could have been avoided OR was it a case of many minor decisions?

3. *Out of the ashes of and biochar of Narrogin – a new attempt at biofuels in* WA by Simon Dawkins

QA. Can government incentives alone, in the area of clean energy, produce stated government policy objectives without creating numerous white elephants?

QB. Do international agreements and targets enhance or inhibit good project planning?

4. *White Elephants in Local Government: Australian Municipal Mergers as State Government Failure* by Brian Dollery

QA. How does Australia's system of Commonwealth, State and Local government lead to increasing numbers of white elephant projects?

QB. Are project processes more efficient when centralised or diversified?

5. *The Black Hole of 10BA* by Justin Macdonnell

QA. What are the major disconnects between policy and implementation in this case study?

QB. How does "stakeholder greed" play an integral role in the creation of white elephants?

6. *The $6.2 million Payroll System that cost Queensland $1.25 billion* by Henrico Dolfing

QA. Why does it take so long to address the obvious white elephants in the planning room?

QB. Why are large-scale technological projects more susceptible to becoming white elephant projects?

7. *Whatever Happened to COVIDSafe?* by Steven Schwartz

QA. Define the key stakeholders in creating this white elephant?

QB. How could the project have been better handled in the given environment?

8. *Movie sets and racetracks –fates awaiting airports that aren't wanted. Beware an excess of optimism!* by Paul Hooper

QA. In terms of new airports what underlying conditions are required before wider benefits will materialise?

QB. Should the validity of forecasts and project appraisals be assessed by independent experts?

9. White Elephants of the Sea: Australia's Disastrous Future Submarine Program by Binoy Kampmark

QA. What factors inhibit "learning from past mistakes"?

QB. What strategies could be used to avoid costly errors when commissioning projects that will not be realised until many years later?

10. *"Tell 'him he's dreamin'" The Olympic Games - a case of over-promising and under-delivering* by David Gration

QA. How can you avoid conflicts between major institutionalised stakeholders?

QB. Does enthusiasm for a project, such as the Olympics, justify a "crash or crash-through approach to project management?

244

www.ingramcontent.com/pod-product-compliance
Lightning Source LLC
Chambersburg PA
CBHW061243220326
41599CB00028B/5520